THE STYLE OF J. S. BACH'S CHORALE PRELUDES

By Robert L. Tusler

With a new Preface by the author

A reprint of the 1956 edition

First published in 1956, this monograph was described in glowing terms by David Craighead, dean of the Organ Department at the Eastman School of Music:

> Although written in such a manner as to be readily understood by non-organists, the text provides a valuable reference work for professional and student organists. Of special importance are its succinct chapters on the German baroque organ, on ornamentation, and on rhythmic patterns and melodic figures of the chorale preludes. This latter is probably the most important part of the book, inasmuch as the subject is usually either neglected or presented from the subjective, pictorial standpoint. Ever controversial issues such as tempi and rhythm of ornaments are deftly and convincingly handled. Stressed is the baroque love of tone color and rhythmic vitality. . . . It is indeed a joy that such a book is now generally available.

Clearly a major work, *The Style of J. S. Bach's Chorale Preludes* is well on its way to becoming a standard reference. For the Da Capo Press edition, Professor Tusler, currently Assistant Dean of the College of Fine Arts, University of California at Los Angeles, has written a new Preface which amplifies his original study and brings it up to date. Also included are an Appendix listing the chorale preludes according to type, and an extensive Bibliography, which has been expanded for this edition. The text itself, thoroughly documented and illustrated with numerous musical examples, remains a model of clear and concise scholarship.

THE STYLE OF J. S. BACH'S
CHORALE PRELUDES

Da Capo Press Music Reprint Series
GENERAL EDITOR
FREDERICK FREEDMAN
VASSAR COLLEGE

THE STYLE OF J. S. BACH'S CHORALE PRELUDES

BY ROBERT L. TUSLER

With a new Preface by the Author

𝄞 DA CAPO PRESS • NEW YORK • 1968

A Da Capo Press Reprint Edition

This Da Capo Press edition of *The Style of J. S. Bach's Chorale Preludes* is an unabridged republication of the first edition published in 1956 as Volume 1, Number 2, in the Music Series by the University of California Press. The University of California Press pagination has been retained in this Da Capo Press reprint, in square brackets, to facilitate reference to citations based on that edition.

Library of Congress Catalog Card Number 68-13275

PREFACE

It is a pleasure to see this monograph appear once again. First written as a Master's thesis at UCLA in 1952, it was published as part of the University of California Press Music Series in 1956. It has been a source of encouragement and satisfaction to observe the steadily increasing use of this work by organists, students, and scholars during the past decade.

To look back upon an early effort and to have the opportunity in this preface to evaluate it, to amplify it to some extent, and to correct it, is indeed rewarding. Rewarding, to be sure, but also frustrating, since there is the ever-present realization that so much more could and should be presented; but if that were done, one would have written another book. Yet, a few statements concerning each chapter may help to clarify a number of points and, perhaps, lead the reader to further investigation of the music.

The choice of the large Frauenkirche organ in Dresden to serve as the basis of the discussion in Chapter One has been questioned. That choice was made for the following reasons: The organ was built by one of Germany's greatest organ builders, Silbermann; it realized artistically Baroque aesthetics; it was thought well of by Johann Sebastian Bach and his son Wilhelm Friedemann; and, the principles of tonal and mechanical design represented in the Silbermann organ are basic to Baroque organ design, even in small two-manual instruments with pedals.

At the beginning of the discussion of the Baroque organ, the registration of the chorale prelude, *Auf meinen lieben Gott,* as given by Bach, is mentioned. It should be emphasized that Bach, as well as nearly all other composers of organ music, rarely specified the stops to be employed. Such registrations, therefore, can only be suggestive, for no two organs produce identical qualities of sound, nor do they necessarily have the same stops. The sonorities which can best project the composition must ultimately be determined by the performer at the particular instrument. Concerning the pitch level at which the different lines sound, the performer is expected to understand the particular style and to make his decision without aid of suggested registration.

For the twentieth-century concert organist, registration problems mount continually. He is expected to perform compositions from the entire history of organ literature. At one locale he is confronted with an immense nineteenth-century romantic organ, at another with a twentieth-century classic, and he may even have to adjust to a Hammond electronic instrument. One might compare this musician with a traveling conductor who finds that in each community the instrumentation of the orchestra varies so greatly that it is necessary to reorchestrate every composition. The selection of those qualities of sound which best project the emotional content of the music has been and continues to be one of the organist's major concerns. He must be "all ears," whether performing a chorale prelude by Bach or a mass by Messiaen.

And finally with regard to the Baroque organ, more attention should be given to the concept of terrace-dynamics. All too frequently these words are interpreted to mean only changes of dynamic levels, as in an echo. However, terrace-dynamics is more concerned with changes in quality of sound and textures.

v

The whole concept of terrace-dynamics was interrelated with the concerto principles of the Baroque Era and was thereby a determining factor in the musical structure of the period. The design of organs was also influenced by this all-prevailing principle. Baroque organs were capable of the textural contrasts, quality differentiations, and spatial relations required in the concept of the Baroque concerto.

In the general discussion (Chapter II) of the chorale tunes employed by Bach, it should be mentioned that his choice was influenced by the synod and locale where he served. Bach also chose Lutheran hymns and their tunes that were known in Scandinavia and the Netherlands, as well as throughout Germany. *Allein Gott in der Höh' sei Ehr'* and *Vater unser im Himmelreich* are good examples of tunes which were widely known throughout Europe.

In my discussion of Bach's use of modal melodies, I made the statement that "... [Bach] thereby to some degree has limited himself." I no longer feel this to be accurate and apparently did not in 1952, for the discussions which followed tended to disprove any limitation. Rather than limiting him, the modal melodies which Bach chose seemed to have freed and enriched the harmonies which support the contrapuntal lines. Almost paradoxically, it would seem that Bach frequently found his greatest freedom within restrictions.

In the course of the study, it is implied, though not discussed directly, that the basic organization of the chorale tune is directly related to the surface structure of the chorale prelude. Thus, it is of interest to note the organization of the tunes which Bach chose. That choice is almost equally divided between tunes in bar form (*AAB*) and those which lack a binary structure. Within the bar form, the *A* section of the chosen melody consists of two or three phrases which are repeated; in the *B* section, however, there is considerable variety. The second half of the tune may consist of from two to six phrases (none of which is repeated), or there may be a variation of the second phrase of the *A* section to conclude the melody. Occasionally, the first phrase or its variant will be employed at the end, creating what is sometimes known as a rounded binary form. The following plans will illustrate some of the different bar form organizations.

Ach Gott vom Himmel, sieh darein:	Phrases 1, 2, 1, 2, 3, 4, 5
Allein Gott in der Höh' sei Ehr':	Phrases 1, 2, 1, 2, 3, 4, 2'
Helft mir Gottes Güte preisen:	Phrases 1, 2, 1, 2, 3, 4, 4, 2'
Wachet auf, ruft uns die Stimme:	Phrases 1, 2, 3, 1, 2, 3, 4, 4, 5, 6, 3'

Those tunes which are in a scheme other than binary include: a) a through-composed technique utilizing a length of two to eleven phrases; and b) tunes which repeat phrases in a manner other than bar form. The latter group may consist of only two phrases arranged as in *Christum wir sollen loben schon*, 1, 2, 2', 1', or may have as many as the six phrases forming the plan of *Komm, heiliger Geist*, 1, 2, 3, 4, 5, 2, 3, 4, 6.

In general the chorale prelude follows the structural plan of the borrowed melody, except for those which are of the *free* category (discussed in Chapter III) and for a few instances such as *Wir glauben all' an einen Gott, Schöpfer* (Peters edition IX, p. 62), where only phrases 1, 2, 3, 4, and 11 are used. To study the relationship of the chorale tune's form to the structure of the prelude reveals the phenomenal ingenuity of Johann Sebastian Bach and can only be touched upon very lightly in such a brief space.

Continued research during the past decade on the question of organ compositions employing borrowed melodies has confirmed my original thesis concerning the two categories, *bound* and *free*, and the seven types of chorale preludes discussed in Chapter Three. From *Das Buxheimer Orgelbuch* to the most recent chorale preludes of Johann Nepomuk David, the changing styles can be studied and clarified within the basic seven organizational procedures taken individually or in combinations. This is not to imply, however, that one will find all seven types in *Das Buxheimer Orgelbuch,* or in any given style period, or in the work of any single composer. Most readily traced from the fifteenth through the twentieth century is the *cantus firmus* type, which appears to be the only type which has consistently occurred during the past four hundred years.

On page twenty-five, I pointed out one of Schweitzer's inconsistences but neglected to point out the inaccuracy of his statement: "Towards the end of the Weimar period, however, he becomes independent of his Masters and produces a type of his own — the chorale prelude of the *Orgelbüchlein.*" This implies that the *Orgelbüchlein* is made up of one type of prelude. This is not the case, however, since the collection contains melody chorales, cantus firmus chorales, chorale canons, ornamental chorales, and one chorale fantasia. Thirty of the pieces from the *Orgelbüchlein* are of the melody chorale type and form the bulk of the work. If this type is "the chorale prelude" of the collection, then one need only study Samuel Scheidt's *Mitten in dem Leben* or Friedrich Wilhelm Zachau's *In dulci jubilo* to disprove that Bach "produces a type of his own."

A similar oversimplification was set forth in footnote twenty-four (p. 71) in connection with the chorale motet. I made the statement that Samuel Scheidt was "the originator of this form." Clearly, his teacher, Sweelinck, and other predecessors developed this genre. The temptation to credit any one individual with the creation of a new form in the arts is one which must be avoided. As an acquaintance with the arts grows and matures, their interrelationship becomes increasingly evident; and the proof of any one individual being the originator becomes increasingly difficult to substantiate. The creation of an art work is not an invention or research project, a fact of which we of a technological culture must be ever cognizant.

Chapters Four and Five are summaries which merely introduce the student to some of the complexities of Bach's style. Treatment of harmonic-contrapuntal style (Chapter IV) and ornamentation (Chapter V) was intended to be simple and readily understandable, if not thorough.

Areas which require additional information and comments are numerous, but only some obviously essential points can be cited here. While it is true that ". . . the basic harmonic treatment of the chorale preludes is not original with Bach and clearly shows that he carried on the traditions established by his predecessors" (p. 41), perhaps those traits which make for distinctiveness should have been indicated, as well as some of the specific elements which produce those traits. Are those chord progressions which occur frequently to be considered harmonic formulae? How do standard Baroque chord progressions become the sound of Johann Sebastian? Are his spacing practices so different? What tones are regularly doubled or tripled in a chord? Each trait-complex, so briefly discussed, should be pursued in such a manner in order to arrive at a more fully developed statement.

In the past years many organists have spoken of Chapter Six, *Rhythmic Patterns and Melodic Figures,* as the most helpful in the monograph. If I were to rewrite this section, I would make a sharper distinction between rhythmic patterns and melodic figures by employing the term "pitch formulae" in place of "melodic figures." This term eliminates the rhythmic connotations which the term "melodic figures" contains. It is evident during the discussion that Bach employs rhythmic patterns with differing pitch formulae, thereby creating "melodic figures." The procedure is also reversed in that he will occasionally use a pitch formula with differing rhythmic patterns, thereby employing a type of variation technique which comes down through the centuries.

If the reader will simply substitute "pitch formulae" for "melodic figures," a clearer picture of Bach's creation of motives will emerge. In this day of mathematics, perhaps a simpler formula might be employed: $RP + PF = M$ (Rhythmic Pattern + Pitch Formula = Motive).

The last sentence of the chapter, "Thus, in brief, the style of the chorale preludes may be designated as a figural style," remains true but might well be expanded. This brief statement contains the germ of Bach's use of motives as well as developmental techniques. When one thinks of development, the name of Beethoven first comes to mind, and yet many of the techniques and practices used by that master are already evident in the chorale preludes of Johann Sebastian. To be sure, his style is a figural style, but one must continually remember that it is a constantly developing motival style.

When an attempt is made to find additional important material dealing with the chorale preludes of Bach, the small number of publications to have appeared since 1952 is surprising. Those which might prove of value to the reader are listed on the following pages.

March 15, 1967
Los Angeles

ROBERT L. TUSLER
Assistant Dean, College of Fine Arts
University of California at Los Angeles

SUPPLEMENTARY BIBLIOGRAPHY

Beck, Theodore Albert. *The Organ Chorales of Johann Gottfried Walther: An Analysis of Style.* Doctoral Dissertation: Northwestern University, 1961.

Blount, Gilbert L. *The Use of* Affektenlehre *and* Figurenlehre *in the Organ Chorales of Johann Gottfried Walther.* Master's Thesis: University of California, Los Angeles, 1964.

Bodky, Erwin. *The Interpretation of Bach's Keyboard Works.* Cambridge: Harvard University Press, 1960. [Minor attention to chorale preludes.]

David, K. H. "J. S. Bach 'Aus tiefer Noth schrei' ich zu dir'," *[Neue] Zeitschrift für Musikwissenschaft,* XCVII/10 (Oct., 1930), 802.

Donington, Robert. *Tempo and Rhythm in Bach's Organ Music.* New York: Peters, 1960.

Donington, Robert. *The Interpretation of Early Music,* 2nd ed. London: Macmillan, 1966.

Dufourcq, Norbert. *Jean-Sébastien Bach: Le Maître de L'Orgue.* Paris: Librairie Floury, 1948

Dunham, E. J. "The Schübler Chorales of Johann Sebastian Bach," *Journal of Church Music,* VI/9 (Sept., 1964), 12–13; VI/10 (Oct., 1964), 7–9.

Ehmann, W. "J. S. Bach's 'Dritter Theil der Clavier Uebung' in seiner gottesdienstlichen Bedeutung und Verwendung," *Musik und Kirche,* V (1933), 77.

Eickhoff, Henry John. *The Ritornello Principle in the Organ Works of Johann Sebastian Bach.* Doctoral Dissertation: Northwestern University, 1960.

Emery Walter. "Notes on Bach's Organ Works," *Musical Opinion,* LXXVII/5 (May, 1954), 477.

Emery, Walter. *Notes on Bach's Organ Works: A Companion to the Revised Novello Edition.* London: Novello, 1952–1957. 2 vols.

Gagnebin, Henri. "Les Chorals d'Orgue de J. S. Bach," *Schweizerische Musikzeitung und Sängerblatt,* L/7 (July 15, 1950), 343–346.

Howes, Arthur. "Nun Freut Euch," *Organ Institute Quarterly,* III (Winter, 1953), 32–33.

Howes, Arthur. "Schübler Chorale Preludes," *Organ Institute Quarterly,* V (Spring, 1955), 47–51; V (Winter, 1955), 48–54; VI (Winter, 1956), 40–42.

Hunt, John Eric. *A Companion to Bach's Orgelbüchlein.* London: Compton Organ Co., 1951.

Kathriner, Leo. "Die drei grossen Kyrie-Choräle von J. S. Bach," *Musik und Gottesdienst,* XIII/4 (July/Aug., 1959), 97–108.

Krieger, Erhard. "Die Spätwerke Bachs," *Zeitschrift für Evangelische Kirchenmusik,* VIII (1930), 87.

Moeser, James C. "Symbolism in J. S. Bach's 'Orgelbuechlein'," [master's thesis re-issued serially] (Nov. 1964–July, 1965).

Platen, Emil. *Untersuchungen zur Struktur der chorischen Choralbearbeitung, Johann Sebastian Bachs.* Bonn: Rheinische Friedrich Wilhelms-Universität, 1957.

Schmidt, Warren Frederick. *The Organ Chorales of Johann Gottfried Walther (1684–1748).* Doctoral Dissertation: University of Iowa 1961.

Sexton, E. H. L. "Organ Music Before 1700: with Especial Reference to the Geneology of Bach as a Composer for the Organ," *The Organ,* (XV/57, 13–18; XV/58, 95–101; XV/59, 179–184; XV/60, 230–235; XVI/61, 40–47. XV–XVI/57–61 (1935–1936).
Bach as a Composer for the Organ," *The Organ,* XV–XVI/57–61 (1935–1936). (XV/57, 13–18; XV/58, 95–101; XV/59, 179–184; XV/60, 230–235; XVI/61, 40–47.)

Sumner, William L. *Bach's Organ-Registration.* London: Peters, 1961.

Sumner, William L. "The Organ of Bach," *Eighth Music Book.* Ed. by Max Hinrichsen. London: Hinrichsen, 1956. 14–135.

Suys, Godelieve, and Kamiel d'Hooghe. "De Koraalvoorspelen uit J. S. Bach's 'Orgelbüchlein'", *De Praestant,* V (1956), 81–83.

Tangeman, Robert S. "The Ritornello Forms in Bach's Catechism Chorale Preludes," *Essays on Music in Honor of Archibald Thompson Davison.* Cambridge: Department of Music, Harvard University, 1957. 235–41.

Wishart, Peter. "Bach's Prelude on 'Erbarm Dich'," *Music and Letters,* XXXIII/3 (July, 1952), 215–16.

THE STYLE OF J. S. BACH'S CHORALE PRELUDES

BY

ROBERT L. TUSLER

UNIVERSITY OF CALIFORNIA PRESS
BERKELEY AND LOS ANGELES
1956

University of California Publications in Music
Editors (Los Angeles): H. L. Clarke, W. T. Marrocco, Jan Popper
Volume 1, No. 2, pp. 83–150, 1 figure in text
Submitted by editors September 23, 1955
Issued November 28, 1956

University of California Press
Berkeley and Los Angeles
California

◇

Cambridge University Press
London, England

FOREWORD

MUSICOLOGY is a field to which organists are apt to become addicted. There is nothing strange about this interest when one considers the vast resources of organ literature that culminated in the writings of the immortal Bach. Furthermore, the lack of information and the abundance of misinformation concerning the style of baroque music, especially regarding its performance, prove more than a little challenging to serious students. Unfortunately, in such studies the devotion to accuracy of detail has often appeared to supersede the very music itself. Such is not the case here. For while Mr. Tusler has avoided direct discussions of aesthetics and interpretation per se, the factual material is so presented that the vital, practical aspects of Bach's music are very apparent.

Although written in such a manner as to be readily understood by non-organists, the text provides a valuable reference work for professional and student organists. Of special importance are its succinct chapters on the German baroque organ, on ornamentation, and on the rhythmic patterns and melodic figures of the chorale preludes. This latter is probably the most important part of the book, inasmuch as the subject is usually either neglected or presented from the subjective, pictorial standpoint. Ever controversial issues such as tempi and rhythm of ornaments are deftly and convincingly handled. Stressed is the baroque love of tone color and rhythmic vitality.

Mr. Tusler received his Bachelor of Arts and Bachelor of Music degrees from Friends University, Wichita, Kansas, and his Master of Arts from the University of California, Los Angeles, where he is at present completing his doctorate. He has been a member of the teaching staff at both universities.

Before moving to California he was the organist-choirmaster at St. John's Episcopal Church, Wichita, Kansas, and has held the same position at Grace Lutheran Church, Culver City, California, for the past six years.

It is indeed a joy that such a book is now generally available.

DAVID CRAIGHEAD
Head, Organ Department
Eastman School of Music

Rochester, New York
March 1, 1956

ACKNOWLEDGMENTS

I AM PROFOUNDLY indebted to my teacher and friend, Robert U. Nelson, University of California, Los Angeles, for his wise and patient counsel in preparing this monograph. Appreciation is also due to Laurence Petran and Henry L. Clarke for helpful suggestions and encouragement. Thanks are due to the local editors of the University of California Press and also to Gordon Butcher of the art department of Twentieth Century–Fox Studios.

For permission to quote copyrighted materials, I wish to express my thanks to: The Macmillan Company for quotations from *J. S. Bach* by Albert Schweitzer (copyright, 1950) ; and C. F. Peters Corporation, 373 Fourth Avenue, New York, for musical excerpts from the nine-volume Peters edition of the *Complete Bach Organ Works* (copyright, 1940).

R. L. T.

Los Angeles, California

CONTENTS

INTRODUCTION

NUMEROUS BOOKS and articles have been written concerning Johann Sebastian Bach which deal with almost every aspect of his life, personality, religion, and music. However, it is my opinion that none of the many studies which I know gives a clear summary of Bach's organ style. Many authorities have made statements similar to the following by Paul Henry Lang: "... in spite of the overwhelming bulk of his vocal works Bach's real and most personal domain is instrumental music, especially organ music."[1] And yet few, if any, of these writers have attempted to present a clear and succinct description of his organ style.

Some of the writers who have dealt with only the organ works have become so involved in speculations concerning the emotional and intellectual attitudes expressed, or reasons why Bach wrote certain compositions, that the specific musical factors producing the style have been neglected or possibly taken for granted. This is not to say that suggested intellectual meanings, ideologies, and emotional attitudes are not an integral part of a work of art; but rather that they refer to the aesthetic, and thus highly debatable, aspect of style. In this study I have made an attempt to present a clear summary of Bach's organ style as it may be observed in his chorale preludes. The study is based only upon the purely factual aspect which can be found in the music itself, without the confusion of aesthetic problems which, at best, are personal, unprovable, and unresolvable in the medium of words.[2]

To arrive at a satisfactory understanding of a style in art, no matter in what branch, one must decide upon a definition of the word *style* and proceed from that point. The controversial nature of the meaning of style can readily be seen by the numerous books and articles dealing with the term in various fields of art. From the agreements and disagreements of authorities, such as Guido Adler and C. H. H. Parry, two basic facts are evident: that everything, whether in art or everyday life, has a style of some kind; and that style is necessarily a compound term.

I have found the following definition by Thomas Munro to be most helpful, and have consequently used it as a basis for this study. "A style of art is a compound descriptive type which requires a comparatively large number of specifications for definition. It consists of a combination of traits or characteristics which tend to recur together in different works of art, or have done so in the art of some particular place or period."[3]

Keeping Munro's definition of style in mind, let us now consider the chorale preludes, which will give us, if not a complete understanding of Bach's organ style, at least a most adequate one.

---

[1] For notes, see pp. 71—72.

CHAPTER I

THE BAROQUE ORGAN IN GERMANY

BACH'S KNOWLEDGE of the organ and his ability as a performer were almost legendary. And in the twentieth century his supremacy as composer for the instrument is seldom questioned and rarely, if ever, challenged. It can hardly be disputed that a fine composer has a working knowledge of the instrument for which he is writing, but all too frequently the student or performer does not have a like understanding. Not uncommonly one encounters statements such as the following which indicate either the author's lack of understanding or his lack of interest in the organ:

...counterpoint on the organ is usually quite inarticulate;...though it is often a pleasure to play the organ fugues on the piano, with the aid of a second player, with the unlimited grading of contrapuntal emphasis which the Hammerklavier provides.[4]

Such misunderstandings as this are ample justification for the inclusion of a general chapter dealing with the organ (in particular the baroque organ) in this

Example 1, *a. Auf meinen lieben Gott* (measures 6–8).[5]

study. A comprehension of the mechanical construction and the tonal properties of the instrument will shed considerable light on some of the problems observed in the printed score. Thus in Bach's *Auf meinen lieben Gott* we find the notation given in example 1, *a.* But the sounds of the printed page are not what Bach had in mind, for the actual pitches which he intended are indicated by the registration he suggests at the beginning of the composition: a stop of eight-foot pitch on the first clavier, a sixteen-foot stop on the second clavier, and a four-foot stop in the pedal. The resulting pitch-sounds are indicated in example 1, *b*. Likewise, when the printed page is studied in the light of the registration, it immediately becomes apparent that the cantus firmus is not in the bass but rather in the alto; and that the compass of sound is in reality much larger than the notation would indicate.

From example 1, *a* and *b*, alone it becomes apparent that without a comprehension of the instrument we would be unable to discover and understand all the stylistic traits, and would occasionally be completely misguided as to the actual sound of the music. Without further discussion, therefore, let us now turn to a consideration of the organ in Bach's day.

Example 1, *b*.

The usual location for the organ during the baroque era was in a gallery at the rear of the church. This arrangement allowed for the placing of all pipes and the console in one locale, so that the organist was never separated from his instrument, as he has been in many poorly arranged buildings of later times. In addition, the various divisions spoke into the nave from one direction, providing the organist excellent opportunity to balance and blend his ensemble. The placing of the organ in the gallery also afforded the congregation the finest opportunity for hearing the music, since the gallery provided ample space for the pipes to speak unhampered, and since the rear wall (usually of stone) reflected the tones directly into the nave. Aside from the aural advantages of this arrangement there were visual ones. Organ builders took great pride in beauty of construction. At this time the organ builder was not only expected to build an instrument which was beautiful to hear but also one which was equally inspiring to look upon. In the spaciousness of the gallery the builder gave free rein to his fancy and in many instances created arrangements of pipes and ornamental cases of exquisite beauty.

Within the organ enclosure, the divisions of the organ were generally placed as shown in figure 1. The manuals that controlled the different divisions were named according to the division's location in the enclosure. Thus, since the division occupying the highest level was named Oberwerk, this name was applied to the manual controlling the Oberwerk. The Hauptwerk occupied the central and largest area, and the Brustwerk occupied the lowest position in the enclosure. If

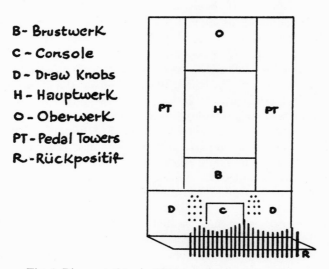

Fig. 1. Diagram of typical baroque organ construction.

a Rückpositif was included, the pipes of this section were placed directly behind the organist at the edge of the gallery, concealing the organist.[6] The number of divisions contained in the instrument determined the number of manuals in the console. The disposition of the manuals varied to some extent excepting the manual controlling the Rückpositif which was always the lowest (1) in the tier of manuals. If there was no Rückpositif then the lowest manual (1) might control the Hauptwerk or the Brustwerk. The following dispositions of manuals were well known to Bach and some were specifically called for in certain of his works: (*a*) I Rückpositif, II Oberwerk, specified by Bach in the "Doric" toccata; (*b*) I Rückpositif, II Oberwerk, III Brustwerk, specified in the Vivaldi-Bach *Concerto in D Minor;* (*c*) I Brustwerk, II Hauptwerk, III Oberwerk, a Silbermann disposition; (*d*) I Rückpositif, II Hauptwerk, III Oberwerk, IV Brustwerk, a Schnitger disposition.

In the twentieth century the average three-manual organ has a console, controlled by electrical contacts, which is separated from the actual mechanism of the pipes. The console is generally built in a modified horseshoe shape, with the manuals in the center and the draw knobs banked conveniently in the sides. If one compares this plan with that of the baroque organ, in which the manuals jut out directly from the enclosure and the draw knobs on both sides of the manuals also come straight from the case, it becomes apparent that the arrangement of the baroque console was much the more cumbersome. This arrangement was necessary since the key action used was that known as *tracker action* and the draw knob actually pulled a "slider" into position. The draw-knob resistance depended upon the length of the slider (sometimes as long as fifteen feet) and the weather. Very damp weather may cause the wood to swell; then the resistance may be impossible to overcome. The usual amount of weight required upon the key to operate the tracker action and bring the pipe into sound was "three ounces ... under perfect conditions."[7] If three ounces of weight were required for one pipe, it may easily be imagined how much strength would be needed to play full organ. "Sometimes the organist had to stand on the pedals and throw the weight of his body on the keys to secure a big chord."[8]

Both these mechanical difficulties had considerable influence upon the style of performance and the manner in which Bach conceived the organ works. How did key resistance affect registration? It is very unlikely that anything comparable to our full organ was ever employed, and doubtful that all the stops of the Hauptwerk were drawn for any extended time. Furthermore, few organs of that period had more than one coupler, and when in use the full strength of the manual being coupled to the Hauptwerk was rarely combined with more than one or two ranks of the Hauptwerk. Again, key resistance influenced tempo. If a composition called for a large registration, the composer could not have intended a presto and probably not even an allegro movement. Where Bach has indicated a presto or an allegro vivace such as in the trio sonatas or the concerti, he certainly did not intend anything approaching full organ. On the contrary, he has written the music so that it insists upon a bright, clear, and light registration.

The mechanical difficulty caused by the cumbersome arrangement and resistance of the draw knobs must have made impossible any rapid change of registration on the part of the performer unless he had an assistant. Consequently, the general practice was to set up the registration of the organ for an entire piece and gain the desired variety of volume and tone color by manual changes. From the study of the music and investigation into the instrument of the time I can find no basis for the constant changes of tone color and dynamic level called for by romantic editors and performers of Bach's works.[9]

Having thus far dwelt upon the mechanical problems which have a direct bearing upon the music, I shall turn to the tonal properties of the baroque organ. All divisions, manuals and pedals, were of equal importance, coördinated with one another, and each was provided with an independent ensemble. From the specification lists of various organs of the period one can readily see that these instruments were designed for a variety of color. The generous supply of independent registers which produce upper partials added a seemingly unlimited tonal palette and gave brilliance and clarity to the entire ensemble. One should also remember that the wind pressures were low, allowing the pipes to speak easily and freely, thereby eliminating the hard, driven, strident tone which is so evident in many romantic and modern organs.

For a clear picture of the tonal properties and how they were organized within an instrument, let us consider the specification list shown in example 2. It is the specification for the Frauenkirche organ in Dresden, which was built by Silbermann in 1736, approved by Friedmann Bach, and played by Johann Sebastian in the same year.

Example 2. Frauenkirche Organ[10]

Hauptwerk:	*Oberwerk:*	*Brustwerk:*	*Pedal:*
Prinzipal 16′	Quintaton 16′	Gedackt 8′	Untersatz 32′
Oktave 8′	Prinzipal 8′	Prinzipal 4′	Prinzipalbass 16′
Gambe 8′	Gedackt 8′	Rohrflöte 4′	Posaunenbass 16′
Rohrflöte 8′	Quintaton 8′	Nasat 3′	Oktavbass 8′
Oktave 4′	Oktave 4′	Oktave 2′	Trompetbass 8′
Spitzflöte 4′	Rohrflöte 4′	Gemshorn 2′	Oktavbass 4′
Quinte 3′	Nasat 3′	Quinte 1½′	Claironbass 4′
Oktave 2′	Oktave 2′	Sifflöte 1′	Mixturenbass 6 fach
Terz 1⅗′	Terz 1⅗′	Mixtur 3 fach	
Kornett 4 fach	Mixtur 4 fach	Schalmei 8′	
Mixtur 4 fach	Vox humana 8′		
Cymbel 3 fach	Klarinette 8′		
Fagott 16′			
Trompete 8′			

Nearly all organs of the period, regardless of the country in which they were constructed, were provided with three basic tone colors: diapason, flute, and reed. German builders of the baroque were also experimenting with another tone color, and developed the lovely family of gambas. This light and mellow string tone blended with the other ensembles easily and effectively; it was not at all like the strident, brash gamba tone of our romantic organs in which the organ builders were attempting to imitate the orchestral strings instead of creating a string tone peculiar to the organ. Within the specification (ex. 2), all four of these basic tone colors are found; a breakdown of the specification into the four (beginning with the diapason family) will show how they are arranged and coördinated.

Example 3. The Diapason Family

Hauptwerk:	*Oberwerk:*	*Brustwerk:*	*Pedal:*
Prinzipal 16′	Prinzipal 8′	Prinzipal 4′	Untersatz 32′
Oktave 8′	Oktave 4′	Oktave 2′	Prinzipalbass 16′
Oktave 4′	Oktave 2′	Mixtur 3 fach	Oktavbass 8′
Oktave 2′	Mixtur 4 fach		Oktavbass 4′
Mixtur 4 fach	Terz 1⅗′		Mixturenbass 6 fach
Cymbel 3 fach			
Terz 1⅗′			

From example 3 we see that each division of the organ is adequately supplied with a diapason chorus or ensemble. The term *organum plenum*, which is frequently found in the works of this period, originally consisted of any one of the series (16′, 8′, 4′, or 8′, 4′, 2′, etc.) of this family or even of all of the diapason chorus. The term did not necessarily indicate the use of couplers, for each division, as can be seen from the breakdown, was supplied with a plenum. When coupling was resorted to, the stop drawn on the first manual to be coupled to the second manual was not usually of the same pitch as the second if they were of the same timbre. If they were of differing colors then they might be of the same pitch. This is a practice which organists would do well to follow in the registration of organ literature from any period.

Diapasons form the heart and center about which the other tone colors group themselves. In the Frauenkirche specification we see twenty of the forty-four ranks belonging to this family; this proportion of diapasons to the other basic colors is common and in many cases considerably larger. It is in this family that the organ builder created either a masterpiece or just another mediocrity. Silbermann accomplished his goal in the Frauenkirche organ and created an instrument that was coördinated by proper distribution of ranks of pipes, by artistic voicing, and by a wind pressure which was fairly low.[11]

Of almost equal importance to the diapason group is the flute family (ex. 4), which in the specification being examined consists of fifteen of the forty-four ranks.

Example 4. The Flute Family

Hauptwerk:	*Oberwerk:*	*Brustwerk:*	*Pedal:*
Rohrflöte 8'	Quintaton 16'	Gedackt 8'	
Spitzflöte 4'	Gedackt 8'	Rohrflöte 4'	
Kornett 4 fach	Quintaton 8'	Nasat 3'	
Quinte 3'	Rohrflöte 4'	Gemshorn 2'	
	Nasat 3'	Quinte 1½'	
		Sifflöte 1'	

Here we have a tone family that is bright, full of charm, and of facile character. For rapid, flowing passages, requiring a certain brilliance, such a chorus of flutes was invaluable, providing the baroque performer with an abundance of light, clear tone from which an accompanimental ensemble could easily be made. And as we shall see later, these registers also served in solo combinations. Frequently during the Bach period the 16', 8', and 4' registers of the flute family were included in the organum plenum to add a little fullness to the ensemble. This would definitely work to advantage when the trumpet ranks were added to the plenum to avoid a too sudden change of quality.

During the baroque period, builders believed in employing a comparatively small portion of the next family, the reed (ex. 5). The distinctive quality of the reeds was developed to its utmost during the nineteenth century; sometimes reeds were used in place of some of the diapason family, such as the mixtures. The baroque attitude is again being expressed to advantage by some twentieth-century builders. The Frauenkirche specification is no exception to the baroque belief, and may be considered as representative.

Example 5. The Reed Family

Hauptwerk:	*Oberwerk:*	*Brustwerk:*	*Pedal:*
Fagott 16'	Vox humana 8'	Schalmei 8'	Posaunenbass 16'
Trompete 8'	Klarinette 8'		Trompetbass 8'
			Clarionbass 4'

In discussing the reeds, Johann Friedrich Agricola states:

The greatest organist and expert on organs in Germany, and perhaps in Europe, the late Kapellmeister Bach, was a friend of the reeds; he for one must have known what could be played on them, and how. Is the convenience of some organists and organ builders really reason enough to scorn such stops, to call them names, and to eliminate them? ... It is known, too, that the famous former organist of this church (St. Catherine's in Hamburg), Mr. Johann Adam Reinken, always kept them in the best tune.[12]

This statement shows that reeds were highly thought of by two of the most eminent organists, but it also indicates that with some this tone family was in disrepute. Why were the reeds in disrepute? First, they were likely to get out of tune easily, thus causing the organist considerable difficulty. Second, because of the low wind pressure they tended to be sluggish in speech, especially if the organ pumper became slack in his duty. And third, the quality of these registers was so individual that it required (and still requires today) careful handling, placing heavy artistic demands upon the performer. It is safe to assume from the individualistic character of these registers that their primary function was that of the solo line; that they were rarely used in the organum plenum, and then only to assist in bringing about a climax in the music.

Just as the reed family was somewhat limited by baroque builders, so was the string family, but even more so. Again, as with the reeds, nineteenth-century builders experimented with and in some cases overdeveloped the string family. In the baroque organ this family (ex. 6) always had the smallest number of ranks (though not generally just one rank), as in the specification we have been studying.

Example 6. The String Family

Hauptwerk: Gambe 8'

In the specification list drawn up by Bach for St. Blasius' Church in Mühlhausen we find the Viol da Gamba 8' called for in the Hauptwerk and the Salicional 4' in the Rückpositif. And from other specification lists of the period, many of which Bach knew well, we find the following ranks of pipes forming the baroque string family: Violon 16', Violon 8', Dulciana 16', Gamba 8', Viol da Gamba 8', Viol da Gamba 4', Salicional 4', and the Violin 2'. The tone produced by these various ranks was generally quite mellow, though certainly not thick and heavy, with a sweetness that added much beauty to the ensemble. Twentieth-century organ builders are once more becoming aware of the real beauty of this family and are gradually eliminating the ugly-sounding imitative gamba registers of the romantic period.

Now that the tonal arrangement has been briefly discussed, the list of combinations in example 7 which were all intended for single-line passages and solo lines, will prove of interest.[13]

Example 7.

Combinations employing diapason and flute tone:

I. Gedackt 8' plus twelfth 2⅔'

II. Nasat 2⅔' plus Oktave 1'

III. Gedackt 8', Oktave 2', Cymbale III

IV. Gedackt 16', Oktave 4', Tierce 1⅗'

V. Bourdon 16', Prinzipal 8', Nasat 2⅔'

Combinations employing diapason and reed tone:

VI. Trumpet 8', Oktave 4'

VII. Vox humana 8', Oktave 4'
VIII. Krummhorn 8', twelfth 2⅔'
IX. Regal 4', Cymbale III
X. Fagotto 16', Oktave 4', Cymbale III

Combinations employing flute and reed tone:
XI. Gedackt 8', Trumpet 4'
XII. Gedackt 16', Trumpet 4'
XIII. Vox humana 8', Gedackt 8', Nasat 2⅔'
XIV. Gedackt 16', Vox humana 8', Flute 4'
XV. Krummhorn 8', Gedackt 8', Nasat 2⅔'

Combinations employing diapason, flute, and reed tone:
XVI. Trumpet 8', Gedackt 8', Oktave 4'
XVII. Vox humana 8', Gedackt 8', Oktave 4'
XVIII. Prinzipal 16', Spitzflöte 8', Trumpet 4'
XIX. Fagotto 16', Quintadena 8', Oktave 4'
XX. Trumpet 16', Nasat 2⅔', Cymbale III

This list of solo combinations is by no means exhaustive, but it serves to show how the tone families were combined to create new and beautiful sounds. From only the twenty combinations cited it is evident that imagination and experimentation were freely employed in the combining of mixtures and mutations with other ranks; and that freedom was given the performer to create vitality deftly within a melodic line and also within the entire ensemble. The Silbermann organ, which I have used as a basis for much of this chapter, affords unlimited possibilities of solo and ensemble combinations, especially when one considers the uniting of ranks within a tone family as well as ranks from the various choruses. Such a wealth of color is common among a large majority of the baroque organs.

Thus, from the foregoing brief discussion of the organs of Bach's time, it becomes evident that an extensive variety of tone quality is one of the baroque organ's chief characteristics. This variety is a significant element in Bach's organ style, an element which was lost sight of by many musicians of romantic and contemporary times. This important element was (and is) neglected not only by organists but also by arrangers of numerous orchestral transcriptions of Bach's organ works. The lack of timbre variety becomes painfully apparent in piano transcriptions which of necessity eliminate this element, and in which the range of sound is compressed into what is the equivalent of only eight-foot registers on the organ. This practice is similar to reducing an orchestral score to a piano score.

In a general fashion this chapter has dealt with those characteristics of the baroque organ which influenced Bach's style. In brief, these influential characteristics are: vast possibilities of differing timbres; an unequaled range of sound; tracker action which eliminates "loud, fast playing"; draw-knob placement and distance, making changes of registration infrequent; independence of each division of the organ, making terrace dynamics an integral part of the style; and a complete lack of percussiveness. With these basic characteristics in mind we are now ready to delve into the more complex and most stimulating traits of Bach's organ style as they are found in the chorale preludes.

CHAPTER II

THE CHORALE TUNE

THE STUDY of baroque organ music must invariably include research into what is probably the core of organ literature in Germany, the chorale prelude. Of all forms of organ music the organ chorale was and is truly *Gebrauchsmusik,* for Protestant organists have constantly employed this type of composition in the service of the church from the time of Sweelinck and Scheidt to the present day. Just as orthodox Lutheranism was deeply imbedded in the life and character of Bach by his environment, so were the chorale and chorale prelude. The affection shown for the chorale was not simply a personal inclination; rather, the chorale was "in the blood of his nation, a prop of their faith, as essential an adjunct of their devotional equipment as the Bible itself."[14]

One can say that Bach began and ended his creative life with the chorales, for since the earliest compositions to which we have access are of this type we may assume, with some sense of surety, that his earliest artistic endeavors were in connection with the chorale. Again, the dictation of the chorale prelude *Vor deinen Thron* to his son-in-law and pupil, Altnikol, brought Bach's creative life to its conclusion.

Bach's devotion to the chorale is shown by the following facts: Well over half of the organ works come under the general category of chorale preludes; there is an almost unlimited use of chorale tunes as the basis of cantatas; chorales are frequently included in the larger choral works such as the *St. Matthew Passion* and the *Christmas Oratorio;* and the chorale tune influenced still other compositions, the most obvious example being the E-flat major fugue, which is based on the first phrase of *Was mein Gott will, das g'scheh Allzeit.*[15]

The majority of the seventy-five tunes which serve as the basis of the 150 chorale preludes and the five chorale partitas are either adaptations of Gregorian chants made by Luther and different composers or original tunes by forerunners of Bach. A few are adaptations of secular songs, such as *Herr Christ, der ein'ge Gottes-Sohn,* which comes from *Ich hört ein Fraulein klagen;* or the familiar *Herzlich thut mich verlangen,* which is an adaptation of Hassler's secular song, *Mein G'müt ist mir verwirret.*

None of the few chorale tunes which Bach composed was used as the basis of an organ composition. Why Bach chose not to use any of his own melodies is difficult to determine conclusively; but some reasons may be gathered from a comparison of the tunes employed and those neglected. Since the chorale prelude was a functional part of the Lutheran worship, congregational familiarity with the chorale melody was important. That the tunes used by Bach were familiar is well illustrated by the numerous settings composed by his predecessors and contemporaries. For example, the melody of *Vater unser im Himmelreich* or that of *Allein Gott in der Höh' sei Ehr'* was set by F. W. Zachau, Andreas N. Vetter, J. G. Walther, Georg Böhm, Samuel Scheidt, and many others. The common congregational tune was the musical element which united the creative genius of Bach with the people of his time. His own chorale tunes did not fulfill this requirement. Further differences between the seventy-five melodies employed by Bach and those not used will become ever more apparent as the characteristics of the various tunes are examined.

Probably one becomes aware first of all of the simple, diatonic, stepwise movement in these melodies. Only occasionally is the stepwise movement interrupted, and then only in favor of the simpler interval: major third, minor third, perfect fourth, perfect fifth, or an octave. No tunes have been used that contain leaps of augmented fourths, diminished fifths, or sevenths, and only five melodies have an interval of a sixth. These five are: *Ein' feste Burg ist unser Gott; Mit Fried' und Freud' ich fahr' dahin; O Mensch, bewein' dein' Sünde gross; Wenn wir in höchsten Nöten sein;* and *Herzlich thut mich verlangen.* In each of them the interval of a sixth occurs only between the last note of a phrase and the first note of the next phrase, never within a phrase. Moreover, each of these melodies has been

Example 8. *Vergiss mein nicht, vergiss mein nicht.*

placed in the upper voice in the chorale prelude and frequently has the leap of the sixth eliminated by additions of ornaments and melodic figures. Thus it is clear that Bach preferred chorales with the simplest melodic intervals, which would become a unifying thread in his tapestry of sound: tunes which would not detract from his own melodic invention and which could readily fit into any voice line.

In striking contrast with the plain chorale melodies which Bach chose to set for the organ are his own tunes with their not infrequent intervals of diminished fifths, sixths, and sevenths. *Vergiss mein nicht, vergiss mein nicht* (ex. 8) provides us with examples of these unwanted intervals.

Another contrasting element may be observed in example 8: that of a range which exceeds an octave. Very few of the seventy-five chosen chorale melodies exceed an octave range, and if they do they exceed it usually by not more than a step. Another point of contrast between the chosen tunes and Bach's is the varying length of phrases, as shown in example 8, when compared to the regularity of the traditional tunes. In general the phrases of the chosen tunes vary from two measures to five measures in length. Usually the chorale tune divides itself into two-, three-, or four-measure phrases throughout; however, it is not difficult to find tunes containing phrases of different lengths. The illustrations in examples 9, 10, and 11 are typical of the tunes in general and clearly demonstrate how the phrases are combined to make the complete tune. The first, *Ach Gott, vom Himmel sieh' darein* (ex. 9), is typical of those tunes which have consistent two-

Example 9. *Ach Gott, vom Himmel sieh' darein.*

measure phrases. Bach has rather consistently chosen for his partitas and for most of the chorales which he arranged more than one or two times tunes that are divided throughout into two-measure phrases, such as *Allein Gott in der Höh' sei Ehr'*, which serves as the foundation for ten chorale preludes. A fairly large number of melodies divide into consistent three-measure phrases, and a few divide into four-measure phrases.

Among the tunes containing phrases of mixed lengths there are two types: those which have the phrase lengths varying consistently in much the same manner as may be observed in *Nun lob', mein' Seel', den Herren* (ex. 10), where an alternation between three- and four-measure phrases occurs, and those of

Example 10. *Nun lob', mein' Seel', den Herren.*

almost complete irregularity, of which *Puer natus in Bethlehem* (ex. 11) is one of the few he chose to set as a chorale prelude.

Another characteristic of the style of the chorale tunes may be observed in these last three examples; that is, the phrases begin on a weak beat of the measure and end on a strong beat (excepting phrase 2 of *Puer natus in Bethlehem*). This is not just a peculiarity of these three tunes, but is generally the rule; in the *371 Harmonized Chorales* we find only 109 of the melodies beginning on the strong beat of the measure. We also find that only one-third of the 150 chorale preludes begin on the strong beat. The following rule seems to apply: If the chorale tune begins with an upbeat, the chorale preludes will do likewise (the only exception being the two settings of *An Wasserflüssen Babylon* in which Bach has changed the meter from ¼ to ¾ and started the prelude on the strong beat); if the chorale tune begins on the strong beat the chorale prelude generally begins on the strong beat.

Example 11. *Puer natus in Bethlehem.*

The idea of progressing from the weak to the strong part of the measure is also seen in the figuration, so that motives and figures almost invariably begin on the weak part of a beat and end on the strong;

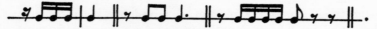

The chorale fugues which have countersubjects consistently, have them entering on the weak part and concluding on the strong part of the beat. This trait is common to the majority of Bach's works whether for organ or not; however, it is one of the basic elements of the rhythmic style of the organ compositions and will be dealt with in more detail in chapter vi.

The rhythmic style of the chorale tunes is best described by two words: direct and straightforward. Meters are limited to the simple ¾ and ¼; these are generally maintained in the chorale preludes. There are a few compositions in which Bach felt the need to change the meter of the original tune; this is true of the previously mentioned settings of *An Wasserflüssen Babylon* and the large and small arrangements for the Catechism Chorales of *Dies sind die heil'gen zehn Gebot.* The latter chorale had as its original meter ¼; this Bach changed to 6/4 for the large catechism chorale and to 12/8 for the smaller (the latter becoming a sprightly gigue fugue for the manuals).

One can hardly say that the chorale tunes are rhythmically interesting, and in no instance are they rhythmically exciting. It would seem that Bach preferred the rhythmically plain and sturdy tune, for all too frequently he would remove any vestige of rhythmic interest when using the melody in a chorale prelude. For example, the original rhythmic motion of *Christ ist erstanden* (ex. 12), though

Example 12. *Christ ist erstanden.*

not great, at least gives some vitality to the line. Example 13 presents it as it is found in the *Orgelbüchlein* chorale prelude completely stripped of any rhythmic interest.

A mere glance at *Ich bin ja, Herr, in deiner Macht* (ex. 14), or almost any of Bach's other original tunes, quickly makes apparent the rhythmic differences be-

Example 13. *Christ ist erstanden.* Vers 1.

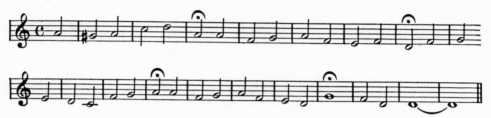

tween them and the chosen seventy-five. Thus again it seems that simplicity (almost to the extent of dullness) is the keynote to the style of the chorale tunes which Bach felt to be suitable for treatment as chorale preludes.

The same lack of complexity which has been characteristic of the various stylistic traits that have been discussed is also in evidence in the tonality of the chorale tunes. A majority of the melodies are in major or minor, and rarely modulate beyond the dominant or the relative major or minor. In general these melodies are such that they do not make specific harmonic-contrapuntal demands. Thus, Bach used the melody, *Jesu meine Freude* (ex. 15), as the basis for the motet by

Example 14. *Ich bin ja, Herr, in deiner Macht.*

the same name, for two chorale preludes, and for six harmonizations in the *371;* in each setting the harmonic-contrapuntal treatment is new and original as if each setting were the first and only.

When Bach employs a modal melody he frequently alters it by an accidental in order to bring it into minor; however, with such tunes as *Aus tiefer Not schrei' ich zu dir* (Phrygian), *Christum wir sollen loben schon* (Dorian), *Das alte Jahr vergangen ist* (Aeolian), and a few others, he has chosen to leave them unaltered and thereby to some degree has limited himself. For by combining these modal melodies with tonal harmonies he can produce only a harmonic scheme similar to that found in the two preludes based on *Christum wir sollen loben schon.* These preludes begin with subdominant harmonies, move to tonic harmonies, and come to a close in the dominant. It is significant that Bach has not composed more than three settings (usually only one or two) of any chorale which is distinctively modal.

The principal stylistic traits of the chorale tune which have been discussed lead to the conclusion that Bach chose those melodies that would generate ideas and

Example 15. *Jesu meine Freude.*

yet be subservient to his musical imagination. The chorale melody is not the composition, nor does the prelude merely support the chorale, but rather the tune is the starting point for a new musical expression and experience. We should keep this in mind in the discussion which follows of the various types of chorale preludes and of how the treatment of the chorale tune determines the type of prelude.

CHAPTER III

THE TYPES OF CHORALE PRELUDES

SPITTA divides Bach's chorale preludes into three categories: pure chorale preludes, organ chorales, and chorale fantasias.[16] The vagueness of these categories becomes all too apparent when one attempts to pin the various preludes down to one of the three, especially since Spitta employs the terms rather freely without making specific exactly what is meant. Somewhat more usable is Schweitzer's classification:

There are three of these [types]. In the first, the whole prelude is constructed out of the motives of the melody, in which case the latter is not altered in any way, but runs through the whole as a *cantus firmus*. This is the "motivistic" method of Pachelbel. In the second, the melody is broken up into arabesques, that climb and wind like a flowering creeper about a simple harmonic stem. This is the "coloristic" method of Böhm. In the third, the melody forms the core of a free fantasia, as in the chorale fantasias of Buxtehude.

All other imaginable kinds of chorale preludes are only intermediate forms between these three main types; we may, for example, in a Pachelbel chorale-fugue, lightly colour and ornament the *cantus firmus*, or weave motives of the melody into the harmonies that support the chorale arabesque in the Böhm style, or, lastly, derive the themes of the Buxtehude fantasia more or less freely from the melody of the chorale.

Bach found these main types and the intermediate forms already in existence. He created no new ones; . . .[17]

What Schweitzer means by the Pachelbel type and the Böhm type is clear, but what he means by the fantasia style of Buxtehude is not. For, earlier, Schweitzer classifies all of Buxtehude's chorale preludes as chorale fantasias and then proceeds to classify Bach's *Herzlich thut mich verlangen* (Peters edition, Vol. V, no. 27) and *Ein' feste Burg* (Peters edition, Vol. VI, no. 22) in the same category of chorale fantasia.[18] Few would disagree with him concerning *Ein' feste Burg*, but I can find no basis for his stating that the four-part harmonization of *Herzlich thut mich verlangen* is in the style of a fantasia. Likewise, it is most confusing and incorrect to classify all Buxtehude's chorale preludes as in the style of a fantasia; one need only study his *Nun komm, der Heiden Heiland* or *Ach Herr, mich armen Sünder*.

Schweitzer himself contradicts his statement on the three types and Bach's having created no new ones: "In the true chorale prelude, Bach appears to have cultivated chiefly the forms of Pachelbel, Böhm, Buxtehude, and Reinken. Towards the end of the Weimar period, however, he becomes independent of his masters and produces a type of his own—the chorale prelude of the *Orgelbüchlein*."[19]

Thus, I feel that Spitta's and Schweitzer's categories are inadequate for the needs of this study. In their place I have chosen two main categories into which all the chorale preludes may be readily placed. First, we have those that are *bound* by the chorale tune, that is, those which employ the tune in its entirety. The cantus firmus chorale, the chorale motet, the chorale canon, the melody chorale, and the ornamental chorale make up this category. Second, those types which treat of only a portion of the tune, that is, the chorale fugue and the chorale fantasia, make up the *free* category.[20] Here the melody may be used variously. For example, the first phrase may be the seed from which the entire prelude develops. This is the usual treatment in the chorale fugues. The opening phrase may serve as the subject of the fugue without alteration, or it may provide the skeleton for a new fugue subject. The chorale prelude *Wir glauben all' an einen Gott, Schöpfer* shows how

the chorale tune phrase  serves as the

skeleton for the subject

Again, the first phrase plus other phrases from the melody, not necessarily in their original order, may form the basis for the composer's free flights of fancy. This is the manner in which the chorale-fantasia type treats the chorale tune. The familiar *In dir ist Freude* is a beautiful example of this type of melodic treatment.

In treating the seven types of preludes I shall deal first with those of the bound category; of these, the *melody chorale* preludes are most numerous.[21] The distinguishing characteristic of this type of chorale prelude is the appearance of the chorale tune as a continuous melody, in virtually its original rhythmic shape, and in the soprano voice. Every detail of the tune is retained in the prelude, the only alteration being the addition of an occasional ornament. Because of this strict adherence to the tune, most of these preludes are short, ranging from ten to twenty measures. When one considers the ten measures of *Ach wie nichtig, ach wie flüchtig* (ex. 16) there is only wonder that so much loveliness and so much of musical interest can be contained in such a brief span of time. The contrapuntal texture

Example 16. *Ach wie nichtig, ach wie flüchtig.*

of this example is no mere accompaniment, but rather the very lifeblood of the composition. Here is a developmental technique that creates a definite mood, provides a climax, and brings the composition to a close with a sense of satisfying completeness. The somewhat bland chorale tune is given a new character by the development of a simple, scalelike figure and a shifting, three-note ostinato. So it is in the majority of the chorale preludes of the melody-chorale type—the contrapuntal texture adds strength and creates interest, always by using one or two melodic figures as the basis of the development.

The majority of the melody chorales are for manuals and pedal, and, as in example 16, the pedal line is of equal importance in the entire texture. Bach was able to express in this type a wide range of emotion, from his most meditative moods to those of great joy. No matter how exuberant the prelude of the melody chorale may be, the virtuoso element is not present; every note is absolutely necessary in these tightly knit pieces; nothing is for display. *Ach wie nichtig, ach wie flüchtig* (ex. 16) is one of the many excellent examples in the *Orgelbüchlein*. Certainly, the prelude is bound by the tune, but the tune is subservient to Bach's musical imagination.

The next most frequently found type of bound chorale prelude is the *cantus firmus*, there being twenty-nine such preludes, plus eight variations from the chorale partitas: *Christ, der du bist der helle Tag,* Variation VII; *Sei gegrüsset, Jesu gütig,* Variations VI, IX, and X; *Vom Himmel hoch da komm' ich her,* Variations I, II, III, and IV. The principal traits of this type are the presentation of the chorale tune generally in long notes and the separation of the phrases of the chorale tune by interludes ranging from one to ten measures in length; the two exceptions are the sixth variation of *Sei gegrüsset, Jesu gütig* and the expressive *Christum wir sollen loben schon.*

In his placement of the cantus, Bach shows a slight preference for the bass. Among the twenty-nine preludes and the three chorale partitas we find thirteen with the cantus in the bass, seven in the tenor, eight in the soprano, four in the alto, and five which have the cantus shifting from one voice to another. Generally, the chorale tune serving as the cantus is without ornamentation; however, there are five chorale preludes which have the cantus ornamented, three of which have the cantus in the tenor[22] *Allein Gott in der Höh' sei Ehr'* (no. 13 of the Great Eighteen) is the only one which employs any extensive ornamentation. This prelude is an excellent example of the incorporation of the principal trait of the ornamental chorale.

Though the cantus firmus chorale is among those classified in the bound category, it shows considerable freedom in the development of the accompanying musical material. The voices may take the form of a two-part invention, a fugue, a motet, a canon, a fantasia, a duet, a trio, or simply furnish an obligato with the pedal providing the continuo. In many instances the accompanying voices are so skillfully worked out in a given form that they constitute a fine composition even with the cantus left out. This is not to say, of course, that the cantus should ever be left out in performance. I shall consider briefly two of these treatments.

The expressive *Christum wir sollen loben schon* from the *Orgelbüchlein* is exceptional not only because the cantus moves continuously throughout but also because this is the only prelude which surrounds the cantus with a trio. The lines flow in such a manner as to enfold the chorale tune in a texture at once rich and crystalline. Imitation, canon, and ornamentation are so deftly employed by the composer that the listener is seldom if ever aware of their presence. One receives the impression, which apparently Bach intended, that the trio serves to enhance the chorale, but is not to be dominated by the chorale tune. A brief quotation (ex. 17) from this prelude can say more than words.

Example 17. *Christum wir sollen loben schon.*

A fugue, usually of three voices, used either below or above the cantus, is one of the most frequently found treatments. One of the most remarkable chorale preludes is *Nun komm' der Heiden Heiland* (no. 11 of the Great Eighteen) which has a carefully worked out three-voiced fugue superimposed on the cantus. The

Example 18.

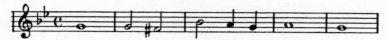

first phrase of the chorale tune (ex. 18) serves as the framework for the fugue subject, as shown in example 19. The exposition of the fugue is presented in the

Example 19.

first eighteen measures, measures 19 through 23 form an episode, and the development section begins in measure 24, at which point the first phrase of the chorale tune, as cantus, makes its entrance. Measures 31 through 38 consist of an episode which leads us to the next entrance of the fugue subject (measures 39–44) and also the second phrase of the cantus. This is followed by a twelve-measure episode (measures 45–56), at which point the third phrase of the cantus appears (measures 57–62). After eighteen more measures of episode the recapitulation of the fugue begins (measure 81) along with the last phrase of the chorale tune. The last note of the cantus provides an eight-measure pedal point which allows the fugue to come to its final cadence. From this brief description we can readily see that the cantus is not the outstanding feature of the composition but rather serves primarily to give the fugue an added sturdiness.

The devices of construction are so numerous in the cantus firmus type of chorale prelude that it is impossible to give them further consideration, even though they hold an almost unlimited wealth of material worthy of study and assimilation. It must suffice to say that within this type one of Bach's most significant stylistic traits is the use of practically all the forms of the baroque in conjunction with a cantus firmus. Let us now consider another type of chorale prelude found in the bound category, the *chorale motet.*

In this type of prelude we find eighteen chorale preludes and none in the variations of the chorale partitas. The principal trait of the chorale motet is the fugal use of all phrases of the chorale tune in their original order. The end result is a series of fugal expositions connected by interludes based on either the phrase just exposed or the oncoming phrase. The majority of these preludes have four voice parts.[23] This particular formation of the prelude is referred to by Spitta as the "pure chorale prelude" and by Schweitzer as the "Pachelbel style"; the latter distinction is correct in the limited sense that Pachelbel used and developed this form to a very high level.[24] However, style is not limited to a form, and when Bach's chorale preludes, which are composed in this form, are referred to as being in the Pachelbel style, considerable confusion can arise. Bach's style in the chorale--motet type of prelude, though similar in form to that of Pachelbel, shows in many of its elements far less similarity to Pachelbel's style than the term implies.

Speaking of the chorale-motet form Schweitzer first considers "Pachelbel's conception of it almost the grandest; . . ."[25] Later Schweitzer says:

With all the excellencies, however, the Pachelbel form of the chorale preludes labour under the grave artistic defect of incoherence. The chorale melody —the bond that should hold together the separate fughettas—cannot really give them intrinsic unity. In the last resort they amount to no more than a string of fragments.[26]

How can this type of prelude be "almost the grandest" and still be incoherent and consist only of a "string of fragments"? I feel that any who have played or listened to the many excellent compositions by Bach and his predecessors written in this manner could hardly agree that they are incoherent. And certainly they do not sound like a "string of fragments" even though they may appear that way on the printed page to one who looks only hastily. Schweitzer's assumption that the chorale melody should be the bond which holds the separate fughettas together is also incorrect. How could the chorale melody be the unifying agent in this form? It is structurally impossible. If the chorale tune should be the unifying factor in this type of prelude, why not in the other types in which the tune is not the unifying element? The answer to this problem is that Bach never uses the chorale tune as the unifying agent but instead depends upon the development of melodic figures and rhythmic patterns to provide coherence. This technique was also practiced by his predecessors and contemporaries, as is well illustrated by Pachelbel's *Herr Gott, dich loben alle wir* (ex. 20).

Twelve Bach preludes of the chorale-motet type employ the chorale melody as a cantus firmus, eleven being found in the soprano and one being found in the first bass part of *Aus tiefer Not schrei' ich zu dir* (Large Catechism Chorale). Except

Example 20. *Herr Gott, dich loben alle wir.*[27]

for *Vater unser in Himmelreich* (Peters, IX, 54), which has the cantus spun out by means of ornamentation, the chorale motets using a cantus firmus present it in long held notes. Generally the phrase of the chorale tune used in each exposition is presented in diminution, but occasionally it is found in its original form.

The other six preludes of the eighteen chorale-motet type have no voice which can be said to act in the manner of a cantus firmus. In these preludes each phrase

Example 21. *Christe, du Lamm Gottes.*

of the chorale melody is presented in a fugue exposition and is generally in its original rhythmic form. Various traits of the chorale fantasia and the ornamental chorale appear in two of these six (*Jesus Christus, unser Heiland, der von uns den Zorn*, no. 16 of the Great Eighteen; and *Komm, heiliger Geist, Herr Gott*, no. 2 of the Great Eighteen). This fact seems to indicate an attempt on Bach's part to enlarge and give a little more freedom to this rather strict form.[28]

Probably the type of prelude which is bound most by the chorale tune is the *chorale canon.* There are twelve chorale preludes of this type and one variation from the chorale partita, *Vom Himmel hoch da komm' ich her* (variation 5). Use of the chorale melody canonically is the distinguishing trait of this type. The eight preludes from the *Orgelbüchlein,* of which example 21 is representative, plus two miscellaneous preludes, have the canon moving continuously throughout the

Example 22. *Dies sind die heil'gen zehn Gebot.*

piece either at the octave or at the fifth. As is shown in example 21, these preludes have, surrounding or supporting the canon, musical material which is developed in the figural manner, as is true of the previously discussed types.

Dies sind die heil'gen zehn Gebot (Large Catechism Chorale) and *Vater unser im Himmelreich* (Large Catechism Chorale) are the two preludes which show an attempt to expand and give freedom to this type of prelude. Both present the phrases of the chorale tune in canon separated by interludes, and each has an introduction which presents the material to be developed in the accompanying voices. Likewise each contains elements of the chorale fantasia. With regard to *Dies sind die heil'gen zehn Gebot* (Large Catechism Chorale), Schweitzer comments:

The symbolism of the great chorale prelude on this catechism-hymn (VI, No. 19), is more profound. It aims at reproducing the dogma of the text. In a lengthy fantasia each of the separate parts goes its own way, without rhythm, without plan, without theme, without regard for the others. This musical disorder depicts the moral state of the world before the law. Then the law is revealed. It is represented by a majestic canon upon the melody of the chorale, running through the whole movement....[29]

Here Schweitzer goes too far in trying to prove the theory of symbolism and using it to explain a composition. If one had never heard or seen this particular work, he would know from Bach's other works that Bach above all was logical and that he would never have written musical lines that "go their own way, without

Example 23. *Wenn wir in höchsten Nöten sein.*

rhythm, without plan, without theme, without regard for the others." Such musical disorder certainly could not even depict what Schweitzer claims for it. Schweitzer's interpretation becomes even more untenable after one has studied the composition and discovered how carefully and skillfully two melodic figures have been developed into a contrapuntal texture that is vital and moving. These two voices, which are in the treble, and the canon, which is in the tenor, are supported by a continuo-like bass. Some of this "musical disorder" may be observed in example 22.

The last type of chorale prelude which can be placed in the bound category is the *ornamental chorale*. The distinguishing characteristic of this type is the chorale melody with its elaborate and expressive ornamentation. The tune, sometimes almost unrecognizable because of the profuse ornamentation, is always in the soprano. Generally the melody moves along gracefully without interruption, supported and enhanced by a contrapuntal texture based upon one or more melodic figures and rhythmic patterns. The nine-measured *Wenn wir in höchsten Nöten sein* (ex. 23) illustrates Bach's ornamental style, with a profusely ornamented melody and with the contrapuntal texture based on one figure (in this case the first four notes of the tune).

Of the twelve ornamental chorale preludes, five have a feature of the cantus firmus type, that of separating the phrases of the tune with interludes. The entire contrapuntal texture, as may be seen in example 24, is in the ornamental style;

thus the interludes do not sharply contrast with those sections where the chorale tune appears. Here the lines ebb and flow gently, with an easy, captivating grace.

Within the frame of the ornamental chorale prelude Bach has poured out some of his most profound feelings. One need only study or hear the anguish-filled *O Mensch, bewein' dein' Sünde gross* or the exquisite measures of *Liebster Jesu, wir sind hier* to know with what loving care Bach molded each ornament and figure, and to recognize the sincerity and compassion of this artist.

Example 24. *Allein Gott in der Höh' sei Ehr'* (no. 12 of the Great Eighteen).

With the ornamental chorale the discussion of the bound category of preludes is concluded. The remaining preludes fall in the free category, made up of the chorale fugue and the chorale fantasia. I shall first discuss the *chorale fugue*.

The chief trait of the chorale fugue is that the first phrase of the chorale tune serves as the basis for the fugue subject. Of the twenty chorale fugues there is only one in which the fugue subject is not immediately recognizable as related to the chorale tune. Example 25 illustrates this chorale tune and the subject of the

Example 25. *Allein Gott in der Höh' sei Ehr'* (Large Catechism Chorale).

fugue. Stainton de B. Taylor states that here the fugue subject is "based on a diminution of the first line of the C. F...."[30] This certainly is most difficult to see, and, I venture to say, impossible to hear. The almost complete disregard for the chorale tune is unlike Bach, especially since it was included as a part of the Catechism Chorales. Could this setting of *Allein Gott in der Höh' sei Ehr'* be based on a tune different from that usually found with this hymn?

Allein Gott in der Höh' sei Ehr' and *Wir glauben all' an einen Gott, Schöpfer* are the only chorale fugues which vary from the rest with regard to the use of more than just the first phrase of the tune. The former employs the first phrase as the subject and the fifth phrase of the tune as the second subject of this double fugue. The latter alludes to the second phrase of the tune in its use of the descending tetrachord.

The majority of these fugues range from fourteen to thirty-five measures in length; hence, most of them are miniature fugues consisting mainly of an exposition and some development, and containing only occasionally any recapitulation. Four are definitely large fugues, ranging from 67 to 137 measures; all are typical of Bach except for *Wir glauben all' an einen Gott, Schöpfer* (Large Catechism Chorale). This magnificent prelude has in the upper three voices a skillfully worked out fugue, and is supplied with a pedal that is independent of the fugue. The subject of the fugue is a vigorous treatment of the simple tune, as is shown in example 26. The pedal part shown punctuates the fugue in seven places through-

Example 26. *Wir glauben all' an einen Gott, Schöpfer.*

Chorale tune

Fugue subject

Pedal part

out the course of the piece, six times in the pedal line and once in the manuals partially incorporated into an episode (measures 76–82). It appears on the following degrees of the scale: tonic, dominant, mediant, leading tone, subdominant, mediant, and tonic. The last time it enters it is spun out to ten measures and helps bring the prelude to a close. No other fugue in the entire organ literature of Bach has a pedal part of this type. It is curious that this device was not used more often by the composer, for in this work it is completely satisfactory. The treading, upward push of this pedal line gives a majestic sweep to the entire fugue and gives to the listener and performer a sensation of unlimited strength and power.

Albert Schweitzer has this to say about *Wir glauben all' an einen Gott, Schöpfer:*

It consists of a gentle, almost dreamy fantasia upon the motive of the first line of the chorale text. In order to understand to what extent this music reproduced the *Credo* for Bach, we must bear in mind the definition to which its essence consists in child-like love and trust in the father.[31]

One can only wonder if Schweitzer really believes this sturdy fugue to be an "almost dreamy fantasia." Whether he does or not, he has done a disservice to this powerful expression of Bach's faith which may be "child-like" in its simplicity but is far from "child-like" and "dreamy" in its projection.

We now come to the seventh and last type of chorale prelude, that of the *chorale fantasia*. In this type there are nine preludes and a large number of the variations of the chorale partitas. Freedom in the treatment of the chorale melody is the keynote for this type. Bach may employ the entire melody or even as little as the first few notes of the head of the theme. If he uses more than one phrase of the chorale melody these phrases may or may not be presented in their original shape or order. The phrases and motives from the chorale tune are usually tossed back and forth among the voices and many times completely lose their identity in the midst of the improvisation. A brief quotation (ex. 27) from *Herr Jesu Christ, dich zu uns wend'* provides an excellent example of the chorale fantasia.

Example 27. *Herr Jesu Christ, dich zu uns wend'* (no. 5 of the Great Eighteen).

Elements from the other types of preludes can easily be found among these preludes and variations of the chorale-fantasia type. The prelude may begin as a trio and bring the chorale tune in as a cantus in the last twenty measures, as in *Herr Jesu Christ, dich zu uns wend'* (ex. 27). Or the prelude may take the shape of the chorale-motet type, interspersing inprovisatory passages between the fugal sections and taking the phrases out of their original order, as in *Valet will ich dir geben* (Peters, VII, 53). Without further examples or discussion it is enough to say that the principal element of the chorale fantasia is complete freedom in the treatment of the chorale tune.

From this survey of the various types of chorale preludes we see that Bach created no new forms. Rather, he combined the traditional patterns into new and vital musical expressions which give an impression that here is an original form. The free combining of stylistic elements of the bound with the free category of preludes, the use of a specific trait of a type in conjunction with another type, and the employment of the chorale tune within these forms as primarily the starting point, indelibly stamp the preludes with Bach's musical logic. He has accepted given forms, then molded and experimented with them until they form a solid foundation for his musical imagination. Thus, the new and original treatment of the traditional types of preludes is a significant element of Bach's organ style, and an understanding of this is basic for the comprehension of this style.

CHAPTER IV

HARMONIC-CONTRAPUNTAL STYLE

"BACH LIVED at a time when the declining curve of polyphony and the ascending curve of harmony intersected, where vertical and horizontal forces were in exact equilibrium."[32] A casual acquaintance with the works of baroque composers readily points to the truth of Bukofzer's statement. And the deeper we probe into Bach's organ style as it is shown in the chorale preludes, the more definite becomes the conclusion that the balance of "vertical and horizontal forces" is one of the chief trait-complexes of Bach's style.

As a beginning step in the understanding of this trait-complex let us consider the harmonic style of the chorale preludes. In general one may say that the harmonic treatment given the preludes is more complex and rich than that found in Bach's other organ compositions. A major factor contributing to this complexity is the frequent mixing of the church modes with the major and minor modes. This treatment is of course in keeping with the nature of the chorale tunes themselves, which were for the most part originally modal. A consideration of the harmonic treatment given the modal melody *Christum wir sollen loben schon* in its setting for the *Orgelbüchlein* (ex. 28) will provide some insight into Bach's method of

Example 28. *Christum wir sollen loben schon.*

combining the church modes with the major and minor. In the chorale prelude on this Dorian tune Bach provides the first phrase with a harmonization in D minor which comes at the close of the phrase to a dominant of the dominant (an E-major chord). The second and the third phrases are in relative major (F major); and the last phrase again is in D minor, with the same type of cadence as used in the first. It is usual in the chorale preludes (especially those having modal melodies) for Bach to employ harmonies similar to the above and to bring the prelude to a final cadence on the dominant or on the dominant of the dominant.

Another element of Bach's harmonic style, especially in the bound category of chorale preludes, is the almost constant changing of chords. For example, in the familiar *O Mensch, bewein' dein' Sünde gross* (ex. 29) there is a change of chord or inversion on every eighth note. Between the eighth notes one sees an abundance of nonharmonic tones which, although not altering the basic chords, add variety of color to the basic harmonies. It is only within the preludes in the free category or those that have many of the stylistic traits of the chorale fantasia that we find a measure or more employing only one chord, generally in brilliant toccata-like passages.

Bach's chord vocabulary consists of those chords which are familiar to any beginning student of harmony; that is: major, minor, augmented, and diminished triads, seventh chords, and occasionally a ninth chord. Each of these types can be found in their inverted forms and also in altered forms. Interestingly, more than half of the tonic triads and seventh chords are found in their first inversion. Seventh chords appear in the following frequency (from the most frequent to the exceptional): V_7, II_7, VII_7, III_7, VI_7, and I_7.

Example 29. *O Mensch, bewein' dein' Sünde gross.*

Just as the twentieth-century musician would consider Bach's chord vocabulary somewhat limited, so also would he consider Bach's key usage limited. For among the chorale preludes there can be found no key having more than four flats or sharps (these extremes are reached in three preludes in F minor and one in E major); and the majority are in keys having only one or two sharps or flats. Bach's restricting himself to sixteen key possibilities is understandable if we remember that organs of his time were rarely tuned satisfactorily according to equal temperament and that many were still tuned either by the mean-tone system or according to just intonation. Likewise, modulations within a composition seldom move the tonality beyond its relative major or minor, or its dominant or subdominant. A key restriction which verges on monotony is found in the chorale partitas. In each chorale partita the key and mode are established and remain the same throughout all the variations. The listener does not mind this limitation in the exuberant *Vom Himmel hoch da komm' ich her,* but in the long *Ach, was soll ich sünder machen* (ten variations) the sound of E minor becomes somewhat wearing.

Thus far the basic harmonic treatment of the chorale preludes is not original with Bach and clearly shows that he carried on the traditions established by his predecessors.[33] Though the materials are the same there is a bolder and more distinctive handling of them: a final welding of modal elements with major-minor tonalities, a freer association of triads, a much more frequent use of chords in their first inversion, and finally a harmonic rhythm that moves much more in accord with the basic rhythmic unit. Above all, it is the greater and more consistent application of nonharmonic tones in creating dissonance that stamps these compositions indelibly with Bach's style.

The nonharmonic tones fall into the following kinds, in order of frequency: passing tones (accented and unaccented), suspensions (single, double, and chain), appoggiaturas, neighboring tones, anticipations, escape tones, changing tones, and pedal points (single and double). These types are readily found in the chorale preludes, and are common to music of the period. However, Bach's use of suspensions and pedal points is somewhat different from that of his predecessors and should be mentioned. With regard to suspensions, Bach's use is more frequent and more free. More freedom is found in the resolution of a suspension, for there are many instances of ornamental resolutions. The following quotations will serve to illustrate:

Example 30. Ornamental Resolutions.

The greater freedom arises from the fact that Bach makes the dissonance produced by the suspension much harsher, and frequently has one dissonance following close upon another. The profound *Da Jesus an dem Kreuze stund* (ex. 31) provides examples of dissonances produced by chain suspensions which create an atmosphere charged with suffering and pain. Likewise, the suspensions plus

Example 31. *Da Jesus an dem Kreuze stund (Orgelbüchlein).*

the chromaticism of *Christus, der uns selig macht* (ex. 32) form dissonances that express a grief which could never be considered sentimental but only strong and powerful, an emotional expression that allows no excess but rather submits to the beauty of restraint. Again, Bach differs from his predecessors and contemporaries in the placement of the suspension, for a suspension in the soprano line is comparatively rare in the chorale preludes. The great majority of suspensions are in the lower voices, with slightly more being found in the alto than in any other voice.

The organ is the ideal instrument for the employment of suspensions, for once a pipe is brought into speech its tone remains unchanged until the wind supply is cut off. Hence the dissonances of suspensions found in the organ works are far more noticeable than those found in Bach's other clavier compositions. One need only perform the previously mentioned *Da Jesus an dem Kreuze stund* on the piano and then on the organ to perceive the truth of this statement. On the piano, because the tone is quickly dissipated, the pedal line provides merely a kind of harmonic seasoning, but when played on the organ, with its unchanging tone, the suspensions become grinding dissonances that at times dominate the entire texture.

In like manner the organ is unexcelled for the performance of pedal points. Bach's sparing use of this device contrasts considerably with its frequent employment by his predecessors. In only one chorale prelude, *In dulci jubilo, nun singet* (Peters, IX, 50), does he use a pedal point from beginning almost to the end, in much the same manner as Merulo or Pachelbel might do.[34] In general, the pedal

Example 32. *Christus, der uns selig macht (Orgelbüchlein)*.

point or double pedal point appears at the end of the composition and lasts from two to six measures. In only a few preludes does a pedal point appear in the course of the musical development. As would be expected, the pedal point is usually placed in the bass; but Bach uses this device occasionally in each of the melodic parts.

Lest one should think that nonharmonic tones are superimposed mechanically to give flavor and to increase interest, it must be said that they are the result of the counterpoint. Likewise much of the harmony itself is a result of the counterpoint and must be studied from the contrapuntal viewpoint. The most significant fact to be remembered concerning Bach's harmonic style is that the harmony serves primarily as a foundation for the counterpoint. Never in the chorale preludes does the harmony merely support a chorale tune[35] in the manner found in S. S. Wesley's justly famous hymn tune *The Church's One Foundation*. In brief, Bach employs a harmonic-contrapuntal style throughout the chorale preludes. With this in mind I should like to discuss briefly the contrapuntal devices found in these works.

Bach's contrapuntal technique in the chorale preludes employs generally the same devices as are found in his other compositions and in the works of his predecessors and contemporaries. These devices are imitation, inversion, retrograde, retrograde inversion, augmentation, diminution, stretto, canon, double counterpoint, triple counterpoint, and fugue. Since these devices are so familiar, to discuss them in any detail seems hardly necessary. The devices of retrograde and retrograde inversion are employed very sparingly; the cantus firmus chorale *Jesus Christus, unser Heiland, der von uns den Zorn Gottes wand* (Large Catechism Chorale) is the only prelude to make extended use of them. Techniques such as quadruple and quintuple counterpoint, crab canon, mirror canon, and mirror fugue are not to be found.

In Bach's works, these devices add variety, or at times tighten up the texture, or expand and develop the musical thought, but they never dominate the composition. For example, in the chorale canons the canon is not allowed to dominate the emotional content but rather gives it support. This is true in *Vater unser im Himmelreich* (Large Catechism Chorale), for we are hardly aware of the canon's presence, because of the vitality of the musical materials surrounding it.[36] A contrapuntal device for Bach is a tool which he uses to express his musical ideas and not something to attract attention to itself.

Lastly, there are two elements of Bach's style which are so common that their importance is often overlooked. The use of sequence and of repetition is so frequent in all of Bach as to make each a major element of his harmonic-contrapuntal style. In the chorale preludes, melodic sequences appear persistently in the bound category of preludes as a part of the development of the melodic figures. A measure of *Herr Christ, der ein'ge Gottes-Sohn* (ex. 33) provides a typical example of Bach's sequencing of melodic figures.

Example 33. *Herr Christ, der ein'ge Gottes-Sohn (Orgelbüchlein).*

Harmonic sequences are found primarily in the free category of preludes, in the interludes of the chorale fantasias, and in the episodes and codettas of the chorale fugues. Although the length of sequence may vary from one to four measures, the average sequence continues for about three measures. Not uncommonly in the large chorale preludes a three-measure sequence is followed immediately by another of the same length to extend the sequential treatment to six measures.

Though the fact is certainly not apparent at first glance, repetition abounds in the chorale preludes, and for that matter in all the organ works. Large sections may be repeated literally, as in the well-known *In dir ist Freude* where measures 1–12 reappear in measures 18–29. Or the repetition of a large section may be disguised by inversion, as in the three-voiced chorale fantasia *Allein Gott in der Höh' sei Ehr'* (Large Catechism Chorale) where measures 1–33 are reproduced in measures 34–66; here the soprano and alto lines are transferred, but the pedal line remains the same. Again we may find two or three voices repeated literally alongside one or two voices of new material.

A particular kind of repetition appears in the melody-chorale type, consisting ordinarily of one or two measures and never of more than a phrase. Generally these small repetitions are separated by at least a phrase of the chorale tune and more often by two or more phrases. *Durch Adam's Fall ist ganz verderbt, Jesus Christus, unser Heiland, der den Tod,* and *In dich hab' ich gehoffet, Herr* from the *Orgelbüchlein* afford excellent examples of small repetitions. Just as a large section may be altered in two or three of its voices upon repetition, so may a measure be repeated with one voice altered. Such repetition occurs frequently in the preludes from the *Orgelbüchlein* and yet when one listens to or performs these powerful expressions of Christian belief the idea of repetition never comes to mind. Bach used repetition to create a unity that is strong yet subtle, but rarely if ever monotonous.

The essence of Bach's harmonic-contrapuntal style is well expressed by Bukofzer:

His melodies have the maximum of linear energy, but are at the same time saturated with harmonic implications. His harmonies have the vertical energy of logical chord progressions, but are at the same time linear in all their voices. Hence, whenever Bach writes harmonically the parts also move independently, and whenever he writes polyphonically the parts move also in tonal harmony.[37]

CHAPTER V

ORNAMENTATION

A SUBSIDIARY factor to Bach's harmonic-contrapuntal style, which was not discussed in the previous chapter because of its complexity, is that of ornamentation. The subject of ornamentation is highly controversial and has been dealt with by numerous authors, not always very helpfully to the performing musician. The following remarks deal only with the types of ornaments found in the chorale preludes, indicating how they have been incorporated into the texture, and in no way attempt an exhaustive discussion of the numerous problems of baroque ornamentation.

Bach did not always leave the interpretation of ornaments to the discretion of the performer; many times he carefully wrote them out. This practice was not typical of the times, and he was adversely criticized for it by some of his contemporaries. Johann Adolph Scheibe said:

But this is impossible. Every ornament, every little grace, and everything that one thinks of as belonging to the method of playing, he expresses completely in notes; and this not only takes away from his pieces the beauty of harmony, but completely covers the melody throughout.[38]

Needless to say, the performing musician of today can be most grateful that Bach did write out the ornaments. For with the aid of the music itself and the explanation of the signs in the *Clavierbüchlein,* written for his son Friedmann, the student of Bach can arrive at some definite ideas concerning Bach's employment of ornaments.

The appoggiatura can easily be termed the principal ornament, for it can be found in almost every prelude either indicated by one of the signs in example 34 or written out.

Example 34.

Bach gives one interpretation of the appoggiatura in Friedmann's *Clavierbüchlein* which is as follows:

Example 35.

In attempting to perform the appoggiaturas which Bach has indicated in the preludes by the symbols, simplicity is the best rule. I know of nothing that leads to more confusion than trying to apply the numerous rules and practices, of which the following are typical, that have been brought to light by the various authorities dealing with this particular ornament:

1. If the main note is dotted, the appoggiatura receives two-thirds of the value.

2. When the main note is tied to the following note, the appoggiatura receives the full value of the first of the tied notes.

3. When the main note forms a dissonance while the appoggiatura forms a consonance with the harmonic structure, then the appoggiatura is short.

4. The appoggiatura is also short when found between repeated notes.

5. It is short also before triplets.

The one rule I have found agreement on which never varies is that the accompanying parts must be played with the first note of the ornament; this is true not merely for the appoggiatura but for all types of ornaments. If this rule is adhered to then of necessity the amount of time required to perform the ornament must be taken from the main note. Since there can be no question that Bach was well aware of the differences in interpretation of the symbols, it would be in keeping with his musical logic to assign the one interpretation given in Friedmann's *Clavierbüchlein* to the symbols and to write out any other type of appoggiatura. Assuming this to be true, I have gone through each prelude containing the appoggiatura symbol and have found that the one interpretation produces the following results.

First, it is in keeping with the harmonic-contrapuntal style of the texture. The quotations found in example 36 and their interpretation clearly show how the appoggiatura provides the nonharmonic tone which is so much a part of Bach's harmonic style and adds to the flow of the melodic line.

Second, this interpretation produces results which are in keeping with the overall rhythmic movement and also with the rhythmic pattern or patterns. This point is readily apparent in example 37.

From example 37 it becomes clear that the interpretation of the appoggiatura symbol according to Friedmann's *Clavierbüchlein* meets the requirements of Bach's harmonic-contrapuntal style and his rhythmic style. The meeting of the requirements of these two principal elements of style is the test for the interpretation of all ornaments and must be strictly adhered to in both study and performance. Before moving on to another type of ornament, a measure (ex. 38) of *Vater unser im Himmelreich* (Large Catechism Chorale), a prelude in which the composer has consistently written out all appoggiaturas, is suggestive.

From the few measures cited it can readily be seen that the appoggiatura is not something added for decoration, but rather that it has been built into the melodic figure and rhythmic pattern.

The mordent is probably the only type of ornament upon which all authorities can agree. The sign, ✦, has been consistently employed by the composers of the period. It is generally conceded that the time required for the small notes must be deducted from the main note and that the mordent is diatonic unless otherwise noted; it is also agreed that the ornament takes the accidentals required by the key and avoids the augmented second when the sixth and seventh degrees in minor are involved. In *Der Tag, der is so freudenreich* (ex. 39) and *Komm, Gott, Schöpfer, heiliger Geist* Bach has incorporated the mordent into the melodic fig-

Example 36. *a. Das alte Jahr vergangen ist.*

b. O Mensch, bewein' dein' Sünde gross.

c. Allein Gott in der Höh' sei Ehr' (no. 12 of the Great Eighteen).

ures and rhythmic patterns of the accompanying parts, the mordent itself providing rhythmic drive.

As with the mordent, the turn has been indicated by one sign, ∾, which on the whole has been interpreted as follows: The turn is diatonic unless otherwise noted; it takes the accidentals of the key; the augmented second is avoided when the sixth and seventh degrees in minor are involved; and the turn always begins with the upper auxiliary unless written ♪♪. Bach's interpretation of the sign ∾ = ♫ is standard. Without difficulty one may find this ornament

Example 37. *Nun komm', der Heiden Heiland* (no. 9 of the Great Eighteen).

Performed

Example 38. *Vater unser im Himmelreich.*

Example 39. *Der Tag, der ist so freudenreich.*

Example 40. *Nun komm', der Heiden Heiland* (no. 9 of the Great Eighteen).

used as the basis of many melodic figures, or written out as in *Nun komm', der Heiden Heiland* (ex. 40), where it gives added push to the melody.

The inverted turn is never indicated in the preludes by a sign, but is always written out as in example 41.

Example 41. *Vom Himmel hoch da komm' ich her.* Variation 5.

Symbols such as ⌐, ⌐, *t*, *tr.* are used indiscriminately by Bach for both the short and long trill. Bach interprets the first sign in this manner:

If we perform this symbol as Bach has indicated, its musical reason comes to the fore, but if it is performed as an inverted mordent (unfortunately heard too frequently) the musical sense is lost. A few examples of both interpretations (ex. 42) will make clear which is preferred within the texture.

Example 42. *a. Gelobet sei'st du, Jesu Christ (Orgelbüchlein).*

b. Liebster Jesu, wir sind hier (Orgelbüchlein).

In the performance of a trill two rules should be observed. The trill should always begin with the note either a half step or a whole above the principal tone; and if the trill is approached from above, the higher note must be restruck or tied over; the trill approached from above is indicated by Bach by means of a slur. Bach either writes out the inverted trill or indicates it by means of a miniature note of the same pitch preceding the main tone.

Let us now consider the remaining types of trills, their symbols, and Bach's interpretation as given in the *Clavierbüchlein:*

Accent and trill (prepared trill)

Trill beginning with a turn or inverted turn

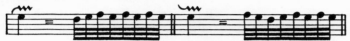

Trill and mordent (trill with suffix)

Double cadence and mordent (trill with appoggiatura, prefix, and suffix)

The various types of trills are ornaments which are frequently neglected or simply ignored by organists, for of all ornaments they require the most careful handling. On the organ the trill played too rapidly becomes a mere blur, and particularly in the high registers creates a buzzing sound that is at times most unpleasant. Otherwise the organist must adjust the speed of his trill to his instrument, with due regard for the acoustics of the building; and what is more important, he must adjust his trill to the rhythmic flow of the individual piece.

The completion of a trill is likely to cause some difficulty, for if precaution is not taken the end result will be false progressions which are definitely not part of the style. No amount of effort is too much to expend in executing the trills properly, for they energize not only the individual melodic lines but the entire texture. The same attitude should be maintained toward all ornaments found in the chorale preludes. The performer should remember that the majority of preludes which are highly ornamented move fairly slowly, with few if any changes of manual; the physical demands are therefore far from impossible.

So, as one labors to bring life to the ornaments which Bach has either written out in full or indicated by a sign, it becomes ever more apparent that no ornament has been used to make the melody "pretty." Rather, the ornaments add to the expressiveness and increase the dramatic intensity and will take their rightful place if the musician frequently examines his interpretation by the two standards mentioned previously: Is the interpretation in keeping with the harmonic-contrapuntal style; and is it in keeping with Bach's rhythmic style?

CHAPTER VI

RHYTHMIC PATTERNS AND MELODIC FIGURES

ONE OF THE strongest elements in all baroque art is motion. Motion, in many instances, seems to be the principal goal of the baroque artist whether he is creating in the medium of sound, color, or stone. In painting the artist gives motion and vitality to his work by play on light and shadow with small details. In architecture he attempts to give the feeling of movement by contrasting masses and using ornaments such as scrolls, statues, and small fantastic figures. No better representative in the field of baroque music can be found than Bach to show this element of motion, for in all his music there is to be found a constant pulsation which relentlessly forces his music forward.[39]

Bach achieves this element in his organ music in spite of what might be considered limitations, that is, the instrument's lack of percussiveness and its total inability to accent an individual tone (each tone of a rank of pipes being of equal strength). Let us now consider the factors which contribute to the development of this motion.

In the chorale preludes there can always be found a unit, such as a quarter, eighth, or sixteenth note, which moves steadily from the beginning of the piece to the end. This constant flow is sometimes brought about, as in the third variation of the chorale partita, *Sei gegrüsset, Jesu gütig* (ex. 43), by a steady stream of

Example 43. *Sei gegrüsset, Jesu gütig.* Variation 3.

sixteenths in the treble and a similar stream of eighths in the bass. However, such a constant flow is generally achieved by exchange of the rhythmic pattern or patterns among the different voices, as in example 44, from *Herr Christ, der ein'ge Gottes-Sohn (Orgelbüchlein)*.

Example 44. *Herr Christ, der ein'ge Gottes-Sohn (Orgelbüchlein).*

A casual acquaintance with the chorale preludes of the baroque period will indicate that patterns of rhythm such as those in the preceding example are an integral part of the style of Sweelinck, Scheidt, Reinken, J. S. Bach, and the majority of the composers of this period. From among the unlimited number of possibilities for rhythmic patterns, we find Bach limiting himself to comparatively few. The patterns in example 45 are the seeds from which his rhythmic development grows.

Example 45. Basic rhythmic patterns.

These rhythmic patterns, or their augmented or diminished variants, are employed by Bach in three ways: first, a pattern may be chosen and used consistently throughout the course of the prelude; second, two patterns may be chosen and used throughout; and third, three or more patterns may be used throughout. I shall consider the three procedures in the order given above.

The chorale preludes which employ a single pattern are of the bound category, with the exception of two chorale fugues, *Christum wir sollen loben schon* (Peters, V, 9) and *Wir glauben all' an einen Gott, Schöpfer* (Peters, VII, 81). And, more specifically, the largest number are of the melody-chorale type, with considerably fewer belonging to the following types: cantus firmus chorale, chorale canon, and ornamental chorale. None of the chorale-motet type employs a single pattern throughout. Among the variations of the chorale partitas there may be found preludes of the chorale-fantasia type, which employ a single rhythmic pattern, as well as the types of preludes already mentioned.

The rhythmic patterns used when a single pattern pervades a piece (numbers 1 through 13 in example 45) are in general quite simple, usually beginning on the offbeat with notes of shorter time value. Dotted rhythms are at a minimum, as are notes longer than a quarter note. Those rhythmic patterns which tend

toward complexity, such as number 12, ![rhythm notation], are employed as the basis of the rhythmic movement of only one prelude; in contrast, the simple

patterns are frequently used. Rhythmic pattern number 1, ![rhythm notation], is probably the most important of all, for it serves almost half of those preludes employing only one rhythmic pattern and may also be found often among preludes using two or more patterns.

When a pattern such as number 1 is used in various chorale preludes, does it always accompany the same melodic figure? The answer is, of course, no. Pattern number 1 may be found in connection with melodic figures such as those shown

Example 46.

in example 46. These are only a few of the melodic figures which Bach combines with this simple rhythmic pattern. However, when Bach chooses to limit himself to one rhythmic pattern in a prelude he often combines it with one melodic figure, together with its variants. Throughout the twelve measures of *Alle Menschen müssen sterben (Orgelbüchlein)* a single rhythmic pattern and a single melodic figure are united and developed into a complete contrapuntal texture. How the pattern is treated during the piece is illustrated by the first four measures of example 47. That is, the alto and tenor voices move melodically and rhythmically parallel, with the pedal always entering later with the same pattern, causing it to overlap. Another characteristic of Bach's rhythmic style may be observed in example 47: that of the lengthening of the last eighth note of the pattern by tying to a sixteenth. This occurs in every measure; it serves the purpose of filling in the harmony and also assures a separation of the pattern from itself.[40]

The range of moods which are expressed by Bach is in no way limited by his confining the contrapuntal texture to one rhythmic pattern and one melodic figure; most often this limitation heightens and clearly defines the emotional content. This becomes apparent from even a casual acquaintance with the joyful and brilliant *In dulci jubilo* or with the meditative *O Lamm Gottes, unschuldig.*

As mentioned before, a rhythmic pattern may have more than one melodic figure associated with it. At the outset of *Heut' triumphieret Gottes Sohn* (ex. 48) Bach distinctly presents two melodic figures, which are in definite contrast melodically but are based upon the same rhythmic pattern. In chorale preludes similar to example 48, the rhythmic pattern clearly acts as one of the unifying agents within the harmonic-contrapuntal texture. Here is one of Bach's solutions

Example 47. *Alle Menschen müssen sterben.*

Example 48. *Heut' triumphieret Gottes Sohn (Orgelbüchlein).*

to the ever-present problem of unity and variety within a musical composition.

It is interesting that within this group of preludes employing one basic rhythmic pattern there should be two chorale fugues, for it is common to find a countersubject with an individual rhythmic pattern in a Bach fugue. In the prelude *Christum wir sollen loben schon* (Peters, V, 9) there is found a consistently used countersubject which, contrary to usual practice, is taken from the conclusion of the subject. In example 49 the relationship between the fugue subject, its countersubject, and the first phrase of the chorale tune may readily be seen. In this ex-

Example 49. *Christum wir sollen loben schon.*

ample, it is clear that the countersubject, although plainly derived from the subject, still complements the subject when combined with it. The second chorale fugue, *Wir glauben all' an einen Gott, Schöpfer*, is probably one of the strongest rhythmically knit fugues that Bach has written. The fugue is based rhythmically and melodically entirely upon a very free version of the first phrase of the chorale tune (ex. 50). Thus it is that Bach creates from this rhythmically potent subject a vital, moving texture.

Example 50. *Wir glauben all' an einen Gott, Schöpfer* (Small Catechism Chorale).

Of all Bach's stylistic traits there is none more significant nor any which more clearly distinguishes his chorale preludes from those of his predecessors and contemporaries, than this of confining a piece to one basic rhythmic pattern and frequently to one melodic figure. The only work which is comparable to Bach in this regard is Buxtehude's partita on *Auf meinen lieben Gott* in which the variations each have a dance rhythm.[41]

More in keeping with the works of his predecessors and contemporaries is the group of chorale preludes which employ two rhythmic patterns. In this group of preludes any pair of rhythmic patterns cited in example 45 may form the core of the motion. Two treatments stand apart from the majority because of their regularity: first, that in which one pattern is employed for the development of musical ideas played on the manuals and a second pattern is used in the pedals as a shifting quasi-ostinato bass; second, that treatment in which one pattern dominates the manuals and the other appears in a regular moving, continuo-like fashion.

Some of the preludes in which the first of these treatments has been employed are: *Ach wie nichtig, ach wie flüchtig; Erstanden ist der heil'ge Christ; Herr Gott, nun schleuss den Himmel auf; Mit Fried' und Freud' ich fahr' dahin* (all from the *Orgelbüchlein*) ; and *Wir glauben all' an einen Gott, Schöpfer* (Large Catechism Chorale). A consideration of example 51 will bring to light how the

Example 51. *a. Erstanden ist der heil'ge Christ.*

b. Mit Fried' und Freud' ich fahr' dahin.

two patterns have been treated. In example 51 we see the patterns in each prelude combined with such balance that their individuality makes itself felt but never interrupts the flowing movement of the whole. Two characteristics present in example 51 and in all chorale preludes in which this treatment may be observed are: the beginning of the pattern on the weak beat or offbeat and the ending on the beat; and the combining of each pattern with only one melodic figure.

It is Bach's limitation of the rhythmic pattern and melodic figure to one in the manuals with a quasi-ostinato pedal which differentiates his chorale preludes from those of Böhm, from whom Bach acquired the ostinato-pedal idea.

The second treatment of the two-pattern type of chorale prelude, that of one distinct pattern in the manuals and a continuo-like pedal, is even more subtle, and is often difficult for the performer to articulate. Some of the preludes containing this treatment are: *Es ist das Heil uns kommen her; Gott, durch deine Güte; Ich ruf' zu dir, Herr Jesu Christ; Puer natus in Bethlehem* (all from the *Orgelbüchlein*); *Nun freut euch, lieben Christen g'mein* (Peters, VII, 36), and *Sei gegrüsset, Jesu gütig,* variation 3, which is quoted in example 43. The characteristics of this treatment are readily observed in example 52. As shown in this

Example 52. *a. Es ist das Heil uns kommen her.*

continuo-like pedal

b. Ich ruf' zu dir, Herr Jesu Christ.

continuo-like pedal

example, the rhythmic pattern employed in the manuals is combined with one melodic figure which is developed in various ways in all the preludes of this group. Likewise, the lack of any specific melodic figure in the continuo-like bass is always a characteristic of this particular treatment.

The remaining chorale preludes that have only two rhythmic patterns as the basis of their movement have no distinguishing trait such as those which have just been discussed. Within this group there can be found all the types of preludes contained in the two large categories, bound and free. The two patterns used during the course of the prelude may be combined to form one large single pattern, or be opposed to one another, or be used alternately. Thus, the Large Catechism Chorale *Jesus Christus, unser Heiland, der von uns den Zorn Gottes wand* (a cantus firmus type of prelude) has as the subject of this two-voice fugue a rhythmic pattern of eighth notes, and as its countersubject a pattern of sixteenth notes. The working out of this composition seems to employ these two patterns in every conceivable manner, with the result that there is never a lag in the motion. Upon hearing this brilliant, scherzo-like fugue played on light, bright stops at a quick tempo the listener must be amazed at the ingenuity of Bach and the clarity with which the musical ideas come across.[42]

That a rhythmic pattern can be assigned to more than one melodic figure within a prelude is evident in both the one-pattern group and the two-pattern group. In the chorale fantasia *Valet will ich dir geben* (Peters, VII, 53) one of the patterns of rhythm has been interpreted melodically as follows:

Example 53.

There is no other type of prelude better suited than the chorale fantasia for assigning more than one melodic figure to a rhythmic pattern; and as might be expected it is within this type that this stylistic trait occurs most frequently.

All that has been said thus far concerning the single- and two-pattern usage applies equally to those preludes which contain three or more rhythmic patterns; hence further quotation is unnecessary. Nevertheless, I should like to discuss, because of its sheer beauty, at least one of the preludes which employ three or more rhythmic patterns. The first that comes to mind is the exuberant and, happily, well-known *In dir ist Freude* (ex. 54). Here we see Bach presenting these

four rhythmic patterns almost immediately: (1)

these he proceeds to develop and mold into one of his most vitally rhythmic

Example 54. *In dir ist Freude (Orgelbüchlein).*

compositions. Rhythmic pattern 1 and its melodic figure (which is derived from the first four tones of the chorale tune) move without significant alteration throughout the piece. Rhythmic pattern 2 and its melodic figure move throughout in an ostinato fashion, driving the music forward uncompromisingly to the last bar, always beginning on the weak beat and ending on the strong; this, as we have already seen, is a familiar characteristic of the quasi-ostinato pattern and of the pattern in general. Rhythmic pattern 3 is also ever present, but clothed in varying

melodic garb that constantly creates new interest and activity within the harmonic-contrapuntal texture. The different melodic figures used with rhythmic

Example 55.

pattern 3 are shown in example 55. Similar to pattern 3 but not so consistently
employed nor so frequently changed melodically is pattern 4. This simple pattern
receives the following melodic changes:

Example 56.

Within *In dir ist Freude* we hear and can see the element of motion at its best.
For here is constant pulsation, contrasting elements, a many-lined texture, alter-
nating with a few-lined texture, a fast-moving harmonic rhythm, and probably
the glittering tinkle of a Cymbelstern. All are combined to create an atmosphere
of irresistible joy.

Just as rhythmic patterns are an essential element of Bach's organ style and of
the style of the majority of baroque composers, so are melodic figures. These
melodic figures stem directly from the figurative techniques of the English vir-
ginalists through Sweelinck and Scheidt to Bach. In the long and splendid history
of the chorale prelude, beginning with Sweelinck's variations on psalm tunes and
chorales, melodic figures have played an important part, sometimes being dealt
with successfully by imaginative composers but all too frequently being handled
so mechanically by less gifted composers as to produce long, dry compositions.
Even Bach's early sets of variations, *Ach, was soll ich Sünder machen* and *O Gott,
du frommer Gott*, suffer from a too mechanical treatment of melodic figures.

From the wealth of melodic figures, which were as much a part of Bach's musical
equipment as were the chorale tunes, Bach again seems to limit himself to a com-
parative few. Bach's basic vocabulary of melodic figures, which appears in example
57, may seem small; however, it should be remembered that they may be augmented, diminished, inverted, used in retrograde or retrograde inversion, or
coupled with a completely different rhythmic pattern.

These basic melodic figures are employed by the composer in much the same
manner as the rhythmic patterns. That is, a single melodic figure may dominate

Example 57.

the contrapuntal texture; two figures may be chosen and used throughout the prelude; or three or more figures may be used.

Within the three ways no one melodic figure is found more frequently than another. Nevertheless, the first ten figures presented in example 57 are the ones most likely to occur in the majority of the chorale preludes. These simple figures may be found separately or in combination with another having more individuality. *Erschienen ist der herrliche Tag* (ex. 58), upon first acquaintance, appears to be so mechanically contrived that it would not bear hearing. But this is hardly true, for Bach's development of this simplest of musical gems is exactly what is needed to break up the rigidity of the canon.

Example 58. *Erschienen ist der herrliche Tag (Orgelbüchlein).*

The complete musical idea of *Allein Gott in der Höh' sei Ehr'* (Peters, VI, 6) is brought about by combining three of the figures in such a manner that the result has a personality of its own (ex. 59).

Example 59. *Allein Gott in der Höh' sei Ehr'.*

When two or more melodic figures are employed to complement each other, Bach logically chooses one which is pliable and one that is assertive. For example, the often mentioned *Durch Adam's Fall ist ganz verderbt (Orgelbüchlein)* has a flowing, scalelike figure weaving in and out of the alto and tenor parts; with this melodic figure Bach has used the sharply contrasting drop of a seventh (major, minor, and diminished) in the pedal with telling results. We have already observed how carefully Bach handles three or more rhythmic patterns; this is equally true when he employs three or more melodic figures. A glance at the previously discussed *In dir ist Freude* (ex. 54) will show how the melodic figures contrast, unite, and alternate, providing a contrapuntal texture that is melodically alive. Or again, a careful study of the chorale motet *Wenn wir in höchsten Nöten sein* (no. 18 of the Great Eighteen) will focus our attention upon the subtle manner in which Bach ties together the fugal sections, which are based upon the phrases of the chorale tune. In this particular prelude Bach has accomplished the smooth flow from one fugue exposition to the next and produced the required sense of unity by weaving into the contrapuntal texture the first melodic figure and its rhythmic pattern. This figure consists of the first four notes of the chorale

tune in diminution:  . Example 60 shows the figure incorporated into the texture of the fugue exposition of the third phrase.

It is most difficult to understand how Schweitzer can say that the chorale-motet form of the chorale prelude is "incoherent" when we see how logically and artistically this prelude is put together. A study of *Komm, heiliger Geist, Herr Gott* (no. 2 of the Great Eighteen), *Aus tiefer Not schrei' ich zu dir* (both the Large and Small Catechism Chorales) or *Ich hab' mein' Sach' Gott heimgestellt*, which are

Example 60. *Wenn wir in höchsten Nöten sein.*

unified in the same manner as *Wenn wir in höchsten Nöten sein,* will clarify once and for all any doubt concerning the coherence of this form.

It was observed above that Bach employs as a melodic figure a part of the chorale tune; this derivation is found not only in the chorale-motet type of prelude but also in the other types. Again I must take exception with Albert Schweitzer because of his very misleading statement concerning this. Speaking of the melody chorale (which, however, he does not call by this name), he says: "In this [type] the melody is used as a *cantus firmus,* unaltered and uninterrupted, usually in the uppermost voice; round it plays an independently conceived motive, not derived from any of the lines of the melody. . . ."[43] It is true that some of the preludes of the type described by Schweitzer have motives which are apparently not derived from any part of the chorale tune; but there are a sufficient number which do have their motives derived from the tune to warrant mentioning them. Thus, in *Christum wir sollen loben schon* (ex. 61) Bach uses a figure clearly derived from the first five tones of the tune. Again, in *Da Jesus an dem Kreuze stund* (ex. 62)

Example 61.
Chorale tune (first phrase)

Melodic figure

we find Bach employing a melodic figure which is derived, although not obviously, from the second phrase of the chorale tune. It is the same melodic figure but coupled with a different rhythmic pattern. And lastly, the beautiful prelude

Example 62.
Chorale tune (second phrase)

Melodic figure

Helft mir Gottes Güte preisen (ex. 63) has an even more clearly derived figure, from the first phrase of the chorale. Without laboring the point further, I mention

Example 63. *Helft mir Gottes Güte preisen.*

the following for additional consideration: *Der Tag, der ist so freudenreich; Gelobet sei'st du, Jesu Christ; Herr Jesu Christ, dich zu uns wend';* and *Nun komm' der Heiden Heiland* (all from the *Orgelbüchlein*).

Thus it is that if we penetrate far enough into the texture of the chorale preludes, we can usually discover a subtle rhythmic or melodic relationship, or a combination of the two. This relationship, in most of the pieces, is felt rather than heard, especially upon first hearing, and does not immediately come to light with the first observance of the score. Nevertheless, as the student and performer of the chorale preludes labors to understand the relationship of Bach's rhythmic patterns and melodic figures to the whole composition, he becomes increasingly aware of the significance of this stylistic trait. It is only through the proper understanding and articulation of the patterns and figures that the performer succeeds in eliminating any possibility of cloudiness and obscurity in the texture and is able to bring forth the inherent power and vitality of the music.

At the conclusion of this study the question may be asked: What in essence is the style of the chorale preludes of Bach? Bach's treatment of rhythmic patterns and melodic figures is the key to an understanding of the style of the preludes; herein lies the force which propels all other elements. This figural treatment, marked by its power to unify and develop musical ideas, distinguishes Bach's preludes from those of his predecessors and contemporaries. Because of Bach's almost rigid adherence to rhythmic patterns and melodic figures, his freest flights of fancy still remain balanced and logical. On the other hand, those preludes which are most bound by the chorale tune are given an improvisatory quality, a sense of freedom, by his careful and subtle development of the patterns and figures into a texture that seems ever fresh and new. Moreover, the figural treatment creates the power which drives the harmonies and contrapuntal lines forward to their goals with energy and clarity.

Thus, in brief, the style of the chorale preludes may be designated as a *figural style*.

APPENDIX
The Chorale Preludes Listed According to Types

MELODY CHORALES

Ach wie nichtig, ach wie flüchtig. Orgelbüchlein, Peters, V, 2.
Alle Menschen müssen sterben. Orgelbüchlein, Peters, V, 2.
Allein Gott in der Höh' sei Ehr'. Peters, IX, 45.
Christ ist erstanden. Orgelbüchlein, Peters, V, 4.
Christ lag in Todesbanden. Orgelbüchlein, Peters, V, 7.
Da Jesus an dem Kreuze stund. Orgelbüchlein, Peters, V, 11.
Der Tag, der ist so freudenreich. Orgelbüchlein, Peters, V, 13.
Dies sind die heil'gen zehn Gebot. Orgelbüchlein, Peters, V, 14.
Durch Adam's Fall ist ganz verderbt. Orgelbüchlein, Peters, V, 15.
Erstanden ist der heil'ge Christ. Orgelbüchlein, Peters, V, 16.
Es ist das Heil uns kommen her. Orgelbüchlein, Peters, V, 18.
Gelobet sei'st du, Jesu Christ. Orgelbüchlein, Peters, V, 19.
Gelobet sei'st du, Jesu Christ. Peters, V, 102.
Helft mir Gottes Güte preisen. Orgelbüchlein, Peters, V, 23.
Herr Christ, der ein'ge Gottes-Sohn. Orgelbüchlein, Peters, V, 24.
Herr Gott, nun schleuss den Himmel auf. Orgelbüchlein, Peters, V, 26.
Herr Jesu Christ, dich zu uns wend'. Orgelbüchlein, Peters, V, 28.
Herr Jesu Christ, dich zu uns wend'. Peters, IX, 50.
Herzlich thut mich verlangen. Peters, V, 30.
Heut' triumphieret Gottes Sohn. Orgelbüchlein, Peters, V, 30.
Ich dich hab' ich gehoffet, Herr. Orgelbüchlein, Peters, V, 35.
Ich ruf' zu dir, Herr Jesu Christ. Orgelbüchlein, Peters, V, 33.
In dulci jubilo. Peters, V, 103.
In dulci jubilo, nun singet. Peters, IX, 50.
Jesu meine Freude. Orgelbüchlein, Peters, V, 34.
Jesus Christus, unser Heiland, der den Tod. Orgelbüchlein, Peters, V, 34.
Liebster Jesu, wir sind hier. Peters, V, 105.
Liebster Jesu, wir sind hier. Peters, V, 39.
Lob sei dem allmächtigen Gott. Orgelbüchlein, Peters, V, 40.
Lobt Gott, ihr Christen, allzugleich. Peters, V, 106.
Lobt Gott, ihr Christen, allzugleich. Orgelbüchlein, Peters, V, 42.
Mit Fried' und Freud' ich fahr' dahin. Orgelbüchlein, Peters, V, 42.
Nun komm' der Heiden Heiland. Orgelbüchlein, Peters, V, 44.
O Lamm Gottes, unschuldig. No. 6 of the Great Eighteen, Peters, VII, 45.
Puer natus in Bethlehem. Orgelbüchlein, Peters, V, 50.
Vater unser im Himmelreich. Orgelbüchlein, Peters, V, 52.
Vater unser im Himmelreich. Small Catechism Chorale, Peters, V, 51.
Vom Himmel hoch da komm' ich her. Orgelbüchlein, Peters, V, 53.
Vom Himmel kam der Engel Schaar. Orgelbüchlein, Peters, V, 54.
Wer nur den lieben Gott lässt walten. Peters, V, 56.
Wer nur den lieben Gott lässt walten. Orgelbüchlein, Peters, V, 57.
Wir Christenleut'. Orgelbüchlein, Peters, V, 58.
Wir danken dir, Herr Jesu Christ. Orgelbüchlein, Peters, V, 59.

CANTUS FIRMUS CHORALES

Ach bleib bei uns, Herr Jesu Christ. Schübler, Peters, VI, 4.
Allein Gott in der Höh' sei Ehr'. Peters, VI, 6.
Allein Gott in der Höh' sei Ehr'. Peters, VI, 8.
Allein Gott in der Höh' sei Ehr'. No. 13 of the Great Eighteen, Peters, VI, 22.
Allein Gott in der Höh' sei Ehr'. Large Catechism Chorale, Peters, VI, 10.
An Wasserflüssen Babylon. No. 3 of the Great Eighteen, Peters, VI, 34.

Christ, unser Herr, zum Jordan kam. Large Catechism Chorale, Peters, VI, 46.
Christum wir sollen loben schon. Orgelbüchlein, Peters, V, 8.
Jesu, meine Freude. Peters, VI, 78.
Jesus Christus, unser Heiland, der von uns den Zorn Gottes wand. Large Catechism Chorale,
    Peters, VI, 82.
Komm, Gott, Schöpfer, heiliger Geist. No. 17 of the Great Eighteen, Peters, VII, 2.
Kommst du nun, Jesus von Himmel herunter. Schübler, Peters, VII, 16.
Kyrie, Christe, aller Welt Trost. Large Catechism Chorale, Peters, VII, 20.
Kyrie, Gott heiliger Geist. Large Catechism Chorale, Peters, VII, 23.
Kyrie, Gott Vater in Ewigkeit. Large Catechism Chorale, Peters, VII, 18.
Meine Seele erhebt den Herren. Schübler, Peters, VII, 33.
Nun freut euch, lieben Christen g'mein. Peters, VII, 36.
Nun freut euch, lieben Christen g'mein. Peters, IX, 52.
Nun komm', der Heiden Heiland. No. 11 of the Great Eighteen, Peters, VII, 42.
Valet will ich dir geben. Peters, VII, 56.
Von Gott will ich nicht lassen. No. 8 of the Great Eighteen, Peters, VII, 70.
Wachet auf, ruft uns die Stimme. Schübler, Peters, VII, 72.
Wer nu den lieben Gott lässt walten. Schübler, Peters, VII, 76.
Wie schon leuchtet der Morgenstern. Peters, IX, 56.
Wir Christenleut. Peters, IX, 60.
Wo soll ich fliehen hin or *Auf meinen lieben Gott. Schübler,* Peters, VII, 84.
Wo soll ich fliehen hin or *Auf meinen lieben Gott.* Peters, IX, 64.

CHORALE MOTETS

Ach Gott, vom Himmel sieh darein. Peters, IX, 42.
Aus tiefer Not schrei' ich zu dir. Large Catechism Chorale, Peters, VI, 36.
Aus tiefer Not schrei' ich zu dir. Small Catechism Chorale, Peters, VI, 38.
Durch Adam's Fall ist ganz verderbt. Peters, VI, 56.
Gelobet sei'st du, Jesu Christ. Peters, VI, 61.
Gottes Sohn ist kommen. Peters, VI, 64.
Ich hab' mein' Sach' Gott heimgestellt. Peters, VI, 74.
Jesus Christus, unser Heiland, der von uns den Zorn. No. 16 of the Great Eighteen, Peters,
    VI, 90.
Jesus Christus, unser Heiland, der von uns den Zorn. No. 15 of the Great Eighteen, Peters,
    VI, 87.
Komm, heiliger Geist, Herr Gott. No. 2 of the Great Eighteen, Peters, VII, 10.
Nun danket alle Gott. No. 7 of the Great Eighteen, Peters, VII, 34.
Vater unser im Himmelreich. Peters, IX, 54.
Vater unser im Himmelreich. Peters, VII, 66.
Vom Himmel hoch da komm' ich her. Peters, VII, 58.
Wenn wir in höchsten Nöten sein. No. 18 of the Great Eighteen, Peters, VII, 74.
Wir glauben all' an einen Gott, Schöpfer. Peters, IX, 62.
Wir glauben all' an einen Gott, Schöpfer. Peters, VII, 82.

CHORALE CANONS

Ach Gott und Herr. Peters, IX, 41.
Auf meinen lieben Gott. Peters, IX, 46.
Christe, du Lamm Gottes. Orgelbüchlein, Peters, V, 3.
Christus, der uns selig macht. Orgelbüchlein, Peters, V, 10.
Dies sind die heil'gen zehn Gebot. Large Catechism Chorale, Peters, VI, 50.
Erschienen ist der herrliche Tag. Orgelbüchlein, Peters, V, 17.
Gott, durch deine Güte or *Gottes Sohn ist kommen. Orgelbüchlein,* Peters, V, 20.
Hilf Gott, das mir's gelinge. Orgelbüchlein, Peters, V, 32.
In dulci jubilo. Orgelbüchlein, Peters, V, 38.

Liebster Jesu, wir sind hier. Orgelbüchlein, Peters, V, 40.
O Lamm Gottes, unschuldig. Orgelbüchlein, Peters, V, 46.
Vater unser im Himmelreich. Large Catechism Chorale, Peters, VII, 60.

ORNAMENTAL CHORALES

Allein Gott in der Höh' sei Ehr'. No. 12 of the Great Eighteen, Peters, VI, 26.
An Wasserflüssen Babylon. Peters, VI, 32.
Das alte Jahr vergangen ist. Orgelbüchlein, Peters, V, 12.
Herr Jesu Christ, dich zu uns wend'. Peters, V, 28.
Jesus, meine Zuversicht. Peters, V, 103.
Liebster Jesu, wir sind hier. Peters, V, 105.
Nun komm', der Heiden Heiland. No. 9 of the Great Eighteen, Peters, VII, 38.
Nun komm', der Heiden Heiland. No. 10 of the Great Eighteen, Peters, VII, 40.
O Mensch, bewein' dein' Sünde gross. Orgelbüchlein, Peters, V, 48.
Schmücke dich, o liebe Seele. No. 4 of the Great Eighteen, Peters, VII, 50.
Wenn wir in höchsten Nöten sein. Orgelbüchlein, Peters, V, 55.
Wer nur den lieben Gott lässt walten. Peters, V, 56.

CHORALE FUGUES

Allein Gott in der Höh' sei Ehr'. Peters, VI, 30.
Allein Gott in der Höh' sei Ehr'. Large Catechism Chorale, Peters, VI, 29.
Christ, unser Herr, zum Jordan kam. Small Catechism Chorale, Peters, VI, 49.
Christum wir sollen loben schon. Peters, V, 9.
Das Jesulein soll doch mein Trost. Peters, IX, 49.
Dies sind die heil'gen zehn Gebot. Small Catechism Chorale, Peters, VI, 54.
Gelobet sei'st du, Jesu Christ. Peters, V, 20.
Gottes Sohn ist kommen. Peters, V, 22.
Herr Christ, der ein'ge Gottes-Sohn. Peters, V, 25.
In dich hab' ich gehoffet, Herr. Peters, VI, 94.
Jesus Christus, unser Heiland, der von uns den Zorn. Small Catechism Chorale, Peters, VI, 92.
Kyrie, Christe, aller Welt Trost. Small Catechism Chorale, Peters, VII, 27.
Kyrie, Gott heiliger Geist. Small Catechism Chorale, Peters, VII, 28.
Kyrie, Gott Vater in Ewigkeit. Small Catechism Chorale, Peters, VII, 26.
Lob sei dem allmächtigen Gott. Peters, V, 41.
Magnificat. Peters, VII, 29.
Nun komm' der Heiden Heiland. Peters, V, 45.
Vom Himmel hoch da komm' ich her. Peters, VII, 67.
Wir glauben all' an einen Gott, Schöpfer. Small Catechism Chorale, Peters, VII, 81.
Wir glauben all' an einen Gott, Schöpfer. Large Catechism Chorale, Peters, VII, 78.

CHORALE FANTASIAS

Allein Gott in der Höh' sei Ehr'. Large Catechism Chorale, Peters, VI, 12.
Allein Gott in der Höh' sei Ehr'. No. 14 of the Great Eighteen, Peters, VI, 17.
Aus der Tiefe rufe ich. Peters, IX, 47.
Christ lag in Todesbanden. Peters, VI, 40.
Ein' feste Burg ist unser Gott. Peters, VI, 58.
Herr Jesu Christ, dich zu uns wend'. No. 5 of the Great Eighteen, Peters, VI, 70.
In dir ist Freude. Orgelbüchlein. Peters, V, 36.
Valet will ich dir geben. Peters, VII, 53.
Vom Himmel hoch da komm' ich her. Peters, V, 106.

NOTES

[1] Paul Henry Lang, *Music in Western Civilization* (New York: W. W. Norton & Co., 1941), p. 504.

[2] Musical symbolism, one of the most controversial issues among students of Bach, comes under the category of aesthetics, and therefore is not within the scope of this paper. Likewise, the style of performance, excepting those procedures which are written into the music itself or are proved practices of the baroque epoch, must be omitted.

[3] Thomas Munro, "Style in the Arts," *Journal of Aesthetics and Art Criticism*, V (Dec., 1946), 128.

[4] A. E. F. Dickinson, "Bach's Fugal Art," *Monthly Musical Record* (Oct., 1948), p. 206.

[5] Unless otherwise indicated, all musical examples of the chorale preludes are taken from Johann Sebastian Bach, *Orgelwerke*, ed. by F. C. Griepenkerl, F. Roitzch, and H. Keller (New York: C. F. Peters, 1940); hereafter cited as Peters.

[6] The following definition of Rückpositif gives the impression that it was only a screen, which is misleading: Rückpositif. In German organs of the 16th to the 18th century, a small structure located at the back of the organist, screening him from the nave" (Willi Apel, *Harvard Dictionary of Music* [Cambridge, Mass.: Harvard University Press, 1947], p. 654).

[7] A. C. Delacour De Brisay, *The Organ and Its Music* (New York: E. P. Dutton & Co., 1934), p. 96.

[8] William H. Barnes, *The Contemporary American Organ* (New York: J. Fischer & Brothers, 1930), p. 212.

[9] I feel that most of the suggestions found in H. Heathcote Statham's "The Aesthetic Treatment of Bach's Organ Music," *Proceedings of the Musical Association*, XXVII, 131–161, are unfounded and contrary to Bach's conception of the music.

[10] Gotthold Frotscher, *Die Orgel* (Leipzig: J. J. Weber, 1927), p. 131.

[11] Ernst Flade gives the following account, which sheds light upon the master's attitude concerning the instrument and its builder: "On the occasion of Bach's performance on the newly completed organ of the Frauen-Kirche in Dresden, when Bach made the personal acquaintance of the builder, Silbermann, he patted him on the back and said: 'Your organs are excellent. You are rightly called Silbermann, for your organs have a silver tone and thundering basses. Just keep on'" (Hans T. David and Arthur Mendel, *The Bach Reader* [New York: W. W. Norton & Co., 1945], p. 289).

[12] David and Mendel, *The Bach Reader*, pp. 257–258.

[13] These combinations are taken from directions given by Schlick, Diruta, Antegnati, Praetorius, Scheidt, Mersenne, Couperin, Werckmeister, Silbermann, Gronau, Dom Bedos, and others.

[14] Charles Sanford Terry, *The Music of Bach* (London: Oxford University Press, 1933), p. 18.

[15] Frequently alluded to as the "St. Anne Fugue."

[16] Phillip Spitta, *J. S. Bach*, tr. by Clara Bell and J. A. Fuller Maitland (London: Novello & Co., 1899).

[17] Albert Schweitzer, *J. S. Bach*, tr. by Ernest Newman (New York: The Macmillan Co., 1950), I, 47–48.

[18] *Ibid.*, I, 46.

[19] *Ibid.*, I, 283.

[20] The types of chorale preludes are taken from Willi Apel's *Harvard Dictionary of Music*, p. 534. Apel postulates an eighth type, the chorale variations (partitas), which is not used above; the reason for this omission is that the individual variations of the chorale partitas can be placed in one of the seven types.

[21] Of the 150 preludes there are 43 of the melody-chorale type plus 9 variations from the chorale partitas.

[22] The chorale preludes having the cantus ornamented are: *Kommst du nun, Jesus von Himmel herunter* (Schübler), *An Wasserflüssen Babylon* (no. 3 of the Great Eighteen), *Allein Gott in der Höh' sei Ehr'* (no. 13 of the Great Eighteen), *Wachet auf, ruft uns die Stimme* (Schübler), and *O Lamm Gottes, unschuldig* (no. 6 of the Great Eighteen, verses 1 and 2).

[23] The following are exceptional: *Aus tiefer Not schrei' ich zu dir* (Large Catechism Chorale) is in six parts, with two played by the pedals; *Wir glauben all' an einen Gott, Vater* has five parts, with two in the pedals; *Vom Himmel hoch da komm' ich her* has five parts; *Ach Gott, vom Himmel sieh darein* begins with four voices, gradually adding a fifth and sixth.

[24] Samuel Scheidt is really the originator of this form. See his prelude on *Christ lag in Todesbanden* in Straube's *Choralvorspiele alter Meister*.

[25] Schweitzer, *op. cit.*, I, 42.

[26] *Ibid.*, I, 45.

[27] Hermann Keller, ed. and comp., *Achtzig Choralvorspiele deutscher Meister* (Leipzig: C. F. Peters, 1937), p. 66.

[28] In the appendix may be found a listing of the chorales according to their types.

[29] Schweitzer, *op. cit.*, II, 59.

[30] Stainton de B. Taylor, *The Chorale Preludes of J. S. Bach* (London: Oxford University Press, 1942), p. 88.

[31] Schweitzer, *op. cit.*, II, 60.

[32] Manfred F. Bukofzer, *Music in the Baroque Era* (New York: W. W. Norton & Co., 1947), p. 303.

[33] A brief survey of works by Scheidt, Schütz, Praetorious, Böhm, and others will make it clear that Bach's harmonic style is a fulfillment of their aims.

[34] This prelude is an early work of Bach and in my opinion not worthy of performance.

[35] This is also true of the *371 Harmonized Chorales.*

[36] I have heard performances of preludes like *Vater unser* . . . in which the organist has taken great pains to bring out the canon by means of differentiation of tone color. I find nothing within the style of the music to warrant this treatment, and feel that such fussiness detracts from the performance.

[37] Bukofzer, *op. cit.*, p. 303.

[38] David and Mendel, *The Bach Reader*, p. 238.

[39] For an excellent article which shows clearly how the element of motion is found in all baroque art, see William Fleming, "The Element of Motion in Baroque Art and Music," *Journal of Aesthetics and Art Criticism*, V (Dec., 1946), 121–129.

[40] In using the tie Bach follows the practice of connecting two tones of equal value or a longer one to a shorter one. This is found to be true in all his organ works. One of the rare exceptions may be found in the Large Catechism Chorale *Kyrie, Gott Vater in Ewigkeit* in which he uses the tie as follows:

[41] This set of variations is in reality a suite, for the movements are entitled Double, Sarabande, Courante, and Gigue, and adhere to the rhythmic patterns of those dances.

[42] The difficulties met in playing this composition no doubt are responsible, at least in part, for its infrequent performance; however, statements such as the following may have even more bearing upon such neglect: "It is as if some one were standing on a rolling ship and planting his feet wide apart in order to keep a firm footing. This theme is characteristic rather than musical, and Bach develops it at too great length; the cantus firmus of the melody, that should hold the whole together, is split up into fragments, with long interludes between them. The total effect of the work is thus not organic" (Schweitzer, *J. S. Bach*, II, 61) and "It is certainly the least attractive of the *Clavierübung* pieces, and most difficult to play. Nor is Bach's conception likely to make much impression on the uninitiated hearer" (Taylor, *The Chorale Preludes of J. S. Bach*, p. 73).

[43] Schweitzer, *op. cit.*, I, 283.

BIBLIOGRAPHY

Adler, Guido. "Style-Criticism," *Musical Quarterly*, XX (April, 1934), 172–176.

――――. *Der Stil in der Musik*. Leipzig: Breitkopf und Haertel, 1911. 279 pp.

Aldrich, Putnam. "Bach's Technique of Transcription and Improvised Ornamentation," *Musical Quarterly*, XXXV (Jan., 1949), 26–35.

Apel, Willi. *Harvard Dictionary of Music*. Cambridge, Mass.: Harvard University Press, 1947. 833 pp.

Audsley, George Ashdown. *The Art of Organ Building*. New York: Dodd, Mead & Co., 1905. 2 vols.

――――. *The Organ of the Twentieth Century*. New York: Dodd, Mead & Co., 1919. 519 pp.

Bach, Carl Philippe Emanuel. *Essay on the True Art of Playing Keyboard Instruments*. Tr. by William J. Mitchell. New York: W. W. Norton & Co., 1949. 449 pp.

Bach, Johann Sebastian. *Werke*. Leipzig: Breitkopf und Haertel, 1862–1904. 47 vols. in 60.

――――. *Orgelwerke*. Ed. by F. C. Griepenkerl, F. Roitzch, and H. Keller. New York: C. F. Peters, 1940. 9 vols.

――――. *The Organ Works*. Ed. by C. M. Widor and A. Schweitzer. New York: G. Schirmer 1940. 5 vols.

――――. *The Liturgical Year*. Ed. by A. Riemenschneider. Philadelphia: Oliver Ditson Co., 1933. 138 pp.

――――. *371 Harmonized Chorales and 69 Chorale Melodies with Figured Bass*. New York: G. Schirmer, 1941. 165 pp.

Barnes, William Harrison. *The Contemporary American Organ*. New York: J. Fischer & Brothers, 1930. 341 pp.

Bonnet, Joseph. *Historical Organ Recitals*. New York: G. Schirmer, 1940. 6 vols.

Boughton, Rutland. *Bach, the Master*. New York: Harper and Brothers, 1930.

Buhrman, T. Scott. *Bach's Life*. New York: Organ Interests, 1935. 54 pp.

Bukofzer, Manfred F. *Music in the Baroque Era*. New York: W. W. Norton & Co., 1947. 411 pp.

Burney, Charles. *A General History of Music*. London: Payne and Son, 1782–1789. 4 vols.

Buxtehude, Dietrich. *The Organ Works*. Ed. by Hermann Keller. New York: C. F. Peters, 1939. 2 vols.

Cherbuliez, Antoine E. *Johann Sebastian Bach*. Switzerland: Verlag Otto Walter Aq., 1946. 235 pp.

David, Hans T., and Arthur Mendel. *The Bach Reader*. New York: W. W. Norton & Co., 1945. 429 pp.

De Brisay, A. C. Delacour. *The Organ and Its Music*. New York: E. P. Dutton & Co., 1934. 200 pp.

Dickinson, A. E. F. "Bach's Fugal Art," *Monthly Musical Record*, LXVII–LIXIX (Sept., 1948—Sept., 1949).

Dolmetsch, Arnold. *The Interpretation of the Music of the Seventeenth and Eighteenth Centuries*. London: Novello & Co., 1944. 493 pp.

Dorian, F. *The History of Music in Performance*. New York: W. W. Norton & Co., 1942. 387 pp.

Emery, Walter. "Bach's Ornaments," *Musical Times*, LXXXIX (1948), 14–16; 43–45.

――――. "Bach's Symbolic Language," *Music and Letters*, XXX (Oct., 1949), 345–354.

Ferguson, Donald N. *A History of Musical Thought*. New York: F. S. Crofts & Co., 1935. 563 pp.

Fleming, William. "The Element of Motion in Baroque Art and Music," *Journal of Aesthetics and Art Criticism*, V (Dec., 1946), 121–129.

Forkel, Johann Nikolaus. *J. S. Bach: His Life, Art, and Work*. Tr. by Charles S. Terry. New York: Harcourt, Brace & Co., 1920. 321 pp.

Frere, W. H. "Bach's Vorspiele of 1739," *Music and Letters*, I (1920), 218–224.

Frotscher, Gotthold. *Die Orgel*. Leipzig: J. J. Weber, 1927. 294 pp.

Gannett, Kent. *Bach's Harmonic Progressions*. Philadelphia: Oliver Ditson Co., 1942. 51 pp.

Gleason, Harold. *Method of Organ Playing*. New York: F. S. Crofts & Co., 1944. 250 pp.

Grace, Harvey. *The Organ Works of Bach*. London: Novello & Co., 1922. 319 pp.

Grew, Eva Mary and Sydney. *Bach*. New York: Pellegrini & Cudahy, 1949. 239 pp.

Grout, Donald Jay. "J. S. Bach: An Appreciation," *Music Review*, VI (1945), 131–137.

Herz, Gerhard. *Johann Sebastian Bach im Zeitalter des Rationalismus und der Frühromantik.* Zürich: Zürich Universität, 1935. 48 pp.

———. "Bach's Religion," *Journal of Renaissance and Baroque Music*, I (June, 1946), 124–138.

Hopkins, Edward John. *The Organ, Its History and Construction.* London: R. Cocks, 1855. 596 pp.

Hull, A. Eaglefield. *Bach's Organ Works.* London: Office of "Musical Opinion," 1929. 189 pp.

Keller, Hermann. "Die Sequenz bei Bach," *Bach Jahrbuch*, XXXVI (1939), 33–42.

———. *Die Orgelwerke Bachs.* Leipzig: C. F. Peters, 1948. 228 pp.

———, ed. and comp. *Achtzig Choralvorspiele deutscher Meister, des 17. und 18. Jahrhunderts.* Leipzig: C. F. Peters, 1937. 123 pp.

Klotz, Hans. *Über die Orgelkunst der Gotik, der Renaissance und des Barock.* Kassel: Bärenreiter-verlag, 1934. 415 pp.

———. *Das Buch von der Orgel.* Kassel: Bärenreiter-verlag, 1949. 148 pp.

———. "Bachs Orgeln und seine Orgelmusik," *Musikforschung*, III (1950), 189–203.

Koch, Caspar. *The Organ Student's Gradus ad Parnassum.* New York: J. Fischer & Brothers, 1945. 172 pp.

Kurth, Ernst. *Grundlagen des linearen Kontrapunkts.* Bern: Akademische Buchhandlung von Max Drechsel, 1917. 515 pp.

Lahee, Henry Charles. *The Organ and Its Masters.* Boston: L. C. Page & Co., 1927. 387 pp.

Lang, Paul Henry. *Music in Western Civilization.* New York: W. W. Norton & Co., 1941. 1,030 pp.

Luedtke, Hans. "Sebastian Bach's Choralvorspiele," *Bach Jahrbuch*, I (1918), 1–96.

McHose, Allen Irvine. *The Contrapuntal Harmonic Technique of the Eighteenth Century.* New York: F. S. Crofts & Co., 1947. 433 pp.

Mahrenholz, Christhard. *Die Orgelregister, ihre Geschichte und ihr Bau.* Kassel: Bärenreiter-verlag, 1930. 324 pp.

Maitland, J. A. Fuller. *The Age of Bach and Handel.* Oxford: Clarendon Press, 1902. 362 pp.

———. "The Toccatas of Bach," *Proceedings of the Musical Association*, XXXIX (1912–1913), 45–53.

Meyer, Ernst Hermann. "The Form in the Instrumental Music of the 17th Century," *Proceedings of the Musical Association*, LXV (1938–1939), 45–61.

Müller-Blattau, Joseph. *Johann Sebastian Bach, Leben und Schaffen.* Leipzig: Phillip Reclam, 1935. 77 pp.

Munro, Thomas. "Style in the Arts, a Method of Stylistic Analysis," *Journal of Aesthetics and Art Criticism*, V (Dec., 1946), 128–158.

Parry, C. Hubert H. *Style in Musical Art.* London: The Macmillan Co., 1924. 438 pp.

———. *The Music of the Seventeenth Century.* Oxford: Clarendon Press, 1938. 474 pp.

———. *J. S. Bach, the Story of the Development of a Great Personality.* New York: G. P. Putnam's Sons, 1909. 584 pp.

Pirro, Andre. *Johann Sebastian Bach, the Organist and His Works for the Organ.* Tr. by Wallace Goodrich. New York: G. Schirmer, 1902. 116 pp.

Prunières, Henry. *A New History of Music.* New York: The Macmillan Co., 1943. 413 pp.

Raugel, Felix. *Les Orgues et les Organistes de la Cathédrale de Strasbourg.* Colmar: Editions Alsatia Colmar, 1948. 30 pp.

Salter, Sumner. "The Ornaments in Bach's Organ Works," *Musical Quarterly*, VI (1920), 393–402.

Scheidt, Samuel. *Ausgewählte Werke für Orgel und Klavier.* Ed. by H. Keller. Leipzig: C. F. Peters, 1939. 145 pp.

Scherchen, Hermann. "Johann Sebastian Bach's Last Composition," *Musical Quarterly*, XXVI (Oct., 1940), 467–482.

Schweitzer, Albert. *J. S. Bach.* Tr. by Ernest Newman. New York: The Macmillan Co., 1950. 2 vols.

Shanet, Howard. "Why Did J. S. Bach Transpose His Arrangements?" *Musical Quarterly*, XXXVI (April, 1950), 181–203.

Smith, Leo. *Music of the Seventeenth and Eighteenth Centuries.* London: J. M. Dent & Sons, 1931. 283 pp.

Spitta, Phillip. *J. S. Bach.* Tr. by Clara Bell and J. A. Fuller Maitland. London: Novello & Co., 1899. 3 vols.

Statham, H. Heathcote. "The Aesthetic Treatment of Bach's Organ Music," *Proceedings of the Musical Association,* XXVII (1900–1901), 131–161.

Straube, Karl. *Alte Meister des Orgelspiels.* Leipzig: C. F. Peters, 1904———. 4 vols.

———. *Choralvorspiele alter Meister.* Leipzig: C. F. Peters, 1907. 170 pp.

Sumner, W. L. "The Organ of Bach," *Organ,* XXX (July, 1950), 1–13.

Sutherland, Gordon, "The Schweitzerian Heresy," *Music and Letters,* XXIII (Oct., 1942), 265–289.

Taylor, Stainton de Boufflers. *The Chorale Preludes of J. S. Bach.* London: Oxford University Press, 1942. 226 pp.

Terry, Charles Sanford. *Bach: The Historical Approach.* London: Oxford University Press, 1930. 257 pp.

———. *Bach.* London: Oxford University Press, 1933. 292 pp.

———. *The Music of Bach.* London: Oxford University Press, 1933. 104 pp.

———. *J. S. Bach's Original Hymn-Tunes.* London: Oxford University Press, 1922. 64 pp.

———. *J. S. Bach's Four-Part Chorales.* London: Oxford University Press, 1929.

———. *Bach's Chorales.* Cambridge: Cambridge University Press, 1915, 1917, 1921. 3 vols.

Valentin, Erich. *Die Entwicklung der Tokkata im 17. und 18. Jahrhundert* (bis J. S. Bach). Münster: Heliosverlag G. M. B. H., 1930. 145 pp.

Williams, C. F. A. *Bach.* London: J. M. Dent & Sons, 1910. 218 pp.

———. *The Story of Organ Music.* London: Walter Scott Publishing Co., 1905. 297 pp.

Zingerle, Hans. *Zur Entwicklung der Melodie von Bach bis Mozart.* Baden bei Wien: Verlag Rudolf N. Rohrer, 1936. 51 pp. plus 31 pp. of examples.